The Land Of Little Rain

by

Mary Hunter Austin

The Echo Library 2006

Published by

The Echo Library

Echo Library
131 High St.
Teddington
Middlesex TW11 8HH

www.echo-library.com

Please report serious faults in the text to complaints@echo-library.com

ISBN 1-40680-678-1

TO EVE, "THE COMFORTRESS OF UNSUCCESS"

PREFACE

I confess to a great liking for the Indian fashion of name-giving: every man known by that phrase which best expresses him to whoso names him. Thus he may be Mighty-Hunter, or Man-Afraid-of-a-Bear, according as he is called by friend or enemy, and Scar-Face to those who knew him by the eye's grasp only. No other fashion, I think, sets so well with the various natures that inhabit in us, and if you agree with me you will understand why so few names are written here as they appear in the geography. For if I love a lake known by the name of the man who discovered it, which endears itself by reason of the close-locked pines it nourishes about its borders, you may look in my account to find it so described. But if the Indians have been there before me, you shall have their name, which is always beautifully fit and does not originate in the poor human desire for perpetuity.

Nevertheless there are certain peaks, cañons, and clear meadow spaces which are above all compassing of words, and have a certain fame as of the nobly great to whom we give no familiar names. Guided by these you may reach my country and find or not find, according as it lieth in you, much that is set down here. And more. The earth is no wanton to give up all her best to every comer, but keeps a sweet, separate intimacy for each. But if you do not find it all as I write, think me not less dependable nor yourself less clever. There is a sort of pretense allowed in matters of the heart, as one should say by way of illustration, "I know a man who...," and so give up his dearest experience without betrayal. And I am in no mind to direct you to delectable places toward which you will hold yourself less tenderly than I. So by this fashion of naming I keep faith with the land and annex to my own estate a very great territory to which none has a surer title.

The country where you may have sight and touch of that which is written lies between the high Sierras south from Yosemite—east and south over a very great assemblage of broken ranges beyond Death Valley, and on illimitably into the Mojave Desert. You may come into the borders of it from the south by a stage journey that has the effect of involving a great lapse of time, or from the north by rail, dropping out of the overland route at Reno. The best of all ways is over the Sierra passes by pack and trail, seeing and believing. But the real heart and core of the country are not to be come at in a month's vacation. One must summer and winter with the land and wait its occasions. Pine woods that take two and three seasons to the ripening of cones, roots that lie by in the sand seven years awaiting a growing rain, firs that grow fifty years before flowering,— these do not scrape acquaintance. But if ever you come beyond the borders as far as the town that lies in a hill dimple at the foot of Kearsarge, never leave it until you have knocked at the door of the brown house under the willow-tree at the end of the village street, and there you shall have such news of the land, of its trails and what is astir in them, as one lover of it can give to another.

CONTENTS:

THE LAND OF LITTLE RAIN

East away from the Sierras, south from Panamint and Amargosa, east and south many an uncounted mile, is the Country of Lost Borders. Ute, Paiute, Mojave, and Shoshone inhabit its frontiers, and as far into the heart of it as a man dare go. Not the law, but the land sets the limit. Desert is the name it wears upon the maps, but the Indian's is the better word. Desert is a loose term to indicate land that supports no man; whether the land can be bitted and broken to that purpose is not proven. Void of life it never is, however dry the air and villainous the soil.

This is the nature of that country. There are hills, rounded, blunt, burned, squeezed up out of chaos, chrome and vermilion painted, aspiring to the snow-line. Between the hills lie high level-looking plains full of intolerable sun glare, or narrow valleys drowned in a blue haze. The hill surface is streaked with ash drift and black, unweathered lava flows. After rains water accumulates in the hollows of small closed valleys, and, evaporating, leaves hard dry levels of pure desertness that get the local name of dry lakes. Where the mountains are steep and the rains heavy, the pool is never quite dry, but dark and bitter, rimmed about with the efflorescence of alkaline deposits. A thin crust of it lies along the marsh over the vegetating area, which has neither beauty nor freshness. In the broad wastes open to the wind the sand drifts in hummocks about the stubby shrubs, and between them the soil shows saline traces. The sculpture of the hills here is more wind than water work, though the quick storms do sometimes scar them past many a year's redeeming. In all the Western desert edges there are essays in miniature at the famed, terrible Grand Cañon, to which, if you keep on long enough in this country, you will come at last.

Since this is a hill country one expects to find springs, but not to depend upon them; for when found they are often brackish and unwholesome, or maddening, slow dribbles in a thirsty soil. Here you find the hot sink of Death Valley, or high rolling districts where the air has always a tang of frost. Here are the long heavy winds and breathless calms on the tilted mesas where dust devils dance, whirling up into a wide, pale sky. Here you have no rain when all the earth cries for it, or quick downpours called cloud-bursts for violence. A land of lost rivers, with little in it to love; yet a land that once visited must be come back to inevitably. If it were not so there would be little told of it.

This is the country of three seasons. From June on to November it lies hot, still, and unbearable, sick with violent unrelieving storms; then on until April, chill, quiescent, drinking its scant rain and scanter snows; from April to the hot season again, blossoming, radiant, and seductive. These months are only approximate; later or earlier the rain-laden wind may drift up the water gate of the Colorado from the Gulf, and the land sets its seasons by the rain.

The desert floras shame us with their cheerful adaptations to the seasonal limitations. Their whole duty is to flower and fruit, and they do it hardly, or with tropical luxuriance, as the rain admits. It is recorded in the report of the Death Valley expedition that after a year of abundant rains, on the Colorado desert was found a specimen of Amaranthus ten feet high. A year later the same species in the same place matured in the drought at four inches. One hopes the land may breed like qualities in her human offspring, not tritely to "try," but to do. Seldom does the desert herb attain the full stature of the type. Extreme aridity and extreme altitude have the same dwarfing effect, so that we find in the high Sierras and in Death Valley related species in miniature that reach a comely growth in mean temperatures. Very fertile are the desert plants in expedients to prevent evaporation, turning their foliage edgewise toward the sun, growing silky hairs, exuding viscid gum. The wind, which has a long sweep, harries and helps them. It rolls up dunes about the stocky stems, encompassing and protective, and above the dunes, which may be, as with the mesquite, three times as high as a man, the blossoming twigs flourish and bear fruit.

There are many areas in the desert where drinkable water lies within a few feet of the surface, indicated by the mesquite and the bunch grass (Sporobolus airoides). It is this nearness of unimagined help that makes the tragedy of desert deaths. It is related that the final breakdown of that hapless party that gave Death Valley its forbidding name occurred in a locality where shallow wells would have saved them. But how were they to know that? Properly equipped it is possible to go safely across that ghastly sink, yet every year it takes its toll of death, and yet men find there sun-dried mummies, of whom no trace or recollection is preserved. To underestimate one's thirst, to pass a given landmark to the right or left, to find a dry spring where one looked for running water—there is no help for any of these things. Along springs and sunken watercourses one is surprised to find such water-loving plants as grow widely in moist ground, but the true desert breeds its own kind, each in its particular habitat. The angle of the slope, the frontage of a hill, the structure of the soil determines the plant. South-looking hills are nearly bare, and the lower tree-line higher here by a thousand feet. Cañons running east and west will have one wall naked and one clothed. Around dry lakes and marshes the herbage preserves a set and orderly arrangement. Most species have well-defined areas of growth, the best index the voiceless land can give the traveler of his whereabouts.

If you have any doubt about it, know that the desert begins with the creosote. This immortal shrub spreads down into Death Valley and up to the lower timber-line, odorous and medicinal as you might guess from the

name, wandlike, with shining fretted foliage. Its vivid green is
grateful to the eye in a wilderness of gray and greenish white shrubs.
In the spring it exudes a resinous gum which the Indians of those parts
know how to use with pulverized rock for cementing arrow points to
shafts. Trust Indians not to miss any virtues of the plant world!
Nothing the desert produces expresses it better than the unhappy growth
of the tree yuccas. Tormented, thin forests of it stalk drearily in the
high mesas, particularly in that triangular slip that fans out eastward
from the meeting of the Sierras and coastwise hills where the first
swings across the southern end of the San Joaquin Valley. The yucca
bristles with bayonet-pointed leaves, dull green, growing shaggy with
age, tipped with panicles of fetid, greenish bloom. After death, which
is slow, the ghostly hollow network of its woody skeleton, with hardly
power to rot, makes the moonlight fearful. Before the yucca has come to
flower, while yet its bloom is a creamy cone-shaped bud of the size of a
small cabbage, full of sugary sap, the Indians twist it deftly out of
its fence of daggers and roast it for their own delectation. So it is
that in those parts where man inhabits one sees young plants of *Yucca
arborensis* infrequently. Other yuccas, cacti, low herbs, a thousand
sorts, one finds journeying east from the coastwise hills. There is
neither poverty of soil nor species to account for the sparseness of
desert growth, but simply that each plant requires more room. So much
earth must be preëmpted to extract so much moisture. The real struggle
for existence, the real brain of the plant, is underground; above there
is room for a rounded perfect growth. In Death Valley, reputed the very
core of desolation, are nearly two hundred identified species.
Above the lower tree-line, which is also the snow-line, mapped out
abruptly by the sun, one finds spreading growth of piñon, juniper,
branched nearly to the ground, lilac and sage, and scattering white
pines.

There is no special preponderance of self-fertilized or wind-fertilized
plants, but everywhere the demand for and evidence of insect life. Now
where there are seeds and insects there will be birds and small mammals,
and where these are, will come the slinking, sharp-toothed kind that
prey on them. Go as far as you dare in the heart of a lonely land, you
cannot go so far that life and death are not before you. Painted lizards
slip in and out of rock crevices, and pant on the white hot sands.
Birds, hummingbirds even, nest in the cactus scrub; woodpeckers befriend
the demoniac yuccas; out of the stark, treeless waste rings the music of
the night-singing mockingbird. If it be summer and the sun well down,
there will be a burrowing owl to call. Strange, furry, tricksy things
dart across the open places, or sit motionless in the conning towers of
the creosote.

The poet may have "named all the birds without a gun," but not the
fairy-footed, ground-inhabiting, furtive, small folk of the rainless

regions. They are too many and too swift; how many you would not believe without seeing the footprint tracings in the sand. They are nearly all night workers, finding the days too hot and white. In mid-desert where there are no cattle, there are no birds of carrion, but if you go far in that direction the chances are that you will find yourself shadowed by their tilted wings. Nothing so large as a man can move unspied upon in that country, and they know well how the land deals with strangers. There are hints to be had here of the way in which a land forces new habits on its dwellers. The quick increase of suns at the end of spring sometimes overtakes birds in their nesting and effects a reversal of the ordinary manner of incubation. It becomes necessary to keep eggs cool rather than warm. One hot, stifling spring in the Little Antelope I had occasion to pass and repass frequently the nest of a pair of meadowlarks, located unhappily in the shelter of a very slender weed. I never caught them sitting except near night, but at midday they stood, or drooped above it, half fainting with pitifully parted bills, between their treasure and the sun. Sometimes both of them together with wings spread and half lifted continued a spot of shade in a temperature that constrained me at last in a fellow feeling to spare them a bit of canvas for permanent shelter. There was a fence in that country shutting in a cattle range, and along its fifteen miles of posts one could be sure of finding a bird or two in every strip of shadow; sometimes the sparrow and the hawk, with wings trailed and beaks parted drooping in the white truce of noon.

If one is inclined to wonder at first how so many dwellers came to be in the loneliest land that ever came out of God's hands, what they do there and why stay, one does not wonder so much after having lived there. None other than this long brown land lays such a hold on the affections. The rainbow hills, the tender bluish mists, the luminous radiance of the spring, have the lotus charm. They trick the sense of time, so that once inhabiting there you always mean to go away without quite realizing that you have not done it. Men who have lived there, miners and cattle-men, will tell you this, not so fluently, but emphatically, cursing the land and going back to it. For one thing there is the divinest, cleanest air to be breathed anywhere in God's world. Some day the world will understand that, and the little oases on the windy tops of hills will harbor for healing its ailing, house-weary broods. There is promise there of great wealth in ores and earths, which is no wealth by reason of being so far removed from water and workable conditions, but men are bewitched by it and tempted to try the impossible.

You should hear Salty Williams tell how he used to drive eighteen and twenty-mule teams from the borax marsh to Mojave, ninety miles, with the trail wagon full of water barrels. Hot days the mules would go so mad for drink that the clank of the water bucket set them into an uproar of hideous, maimed noises, and a tangle of harness chains, while Salty

would sit on the high seat with the sun glare heavy in his eyes, dealing
out curses of pacification in a level, uninterested voice until the
clamor fell off from sheer exhaustion. There was a line of shallow
graves' along that road; they used to count on dropping a man or two of
every new gang of coolies brought out in the hot season. But when he
lost his swamper, smitten without warning at the noon halt, Salty quit
his job; he said it was "too durn hot." The swamper he buried by the way
with stones upon him to keep the coyotes from digging him up, and seven
years later I read the penciled lines on the pine headboard, still
bright and unweathered.

But before that, driving up on the Mojave stage, I met Salty again
crossing Indian Wells, his face from the high seat, tanned and ruddy as
a harvest moon, looming through the golden dust above his eighteen
mules. The land had called him.

The palpable sense of mystery in the desert air breeds fables, chiefly
of lost treasure. Somewhere within its stark borders, if one believes
report, is a hill strewn with nuggets; one seamed with virgin silver; an
old clayey water-bed where Indians scooped up earth to make cooking pots
and shaped them reeking with grains of pure gold. Old miners drifting
about the desert edges, weathered into the semblance of the tawny hills,
will tell you tales like these convincingly. After a little sojourn in
that land you will believe them on their own account. It is a question
whether it is not better to be bitten by the little horned snake of the
desert that goes sidewise and strikes without coiling, than by the
tradition of a lost mine.

And yet—and yet—is it not perhaps to satisfy expectation that one
falls into the tragic key in writing of desertness? The more you wish of
it the more you get, and in the mean time lose much of pleasantness. In
that country which begins at the foot of the east slope of the Sierras
and spreads out by less and less lofty hill ranges toward the Great
Basin, it is possible to live with great zest, to have red blood and
delicate joys, to pass and repass about one's daily performance an area
that would make an Atlantic seaboard State, and that with no peril, and,
according to our way of thought, no particular difficulty. At any rate,
it was not people who went into the desert merely to write it up who
invented the fabled Hassaympa, of whose waters, if any drink, they can
no more see fact as naked fact, but all radiant with the color of
romance.

I, who must have drunk of it in my twice seven years' wanderings, am
assured that it is worth while.

For all the toll the desert takes of a man it gives compensations, deep
breaths, deep sleep, and the communion of the stars. It comes upon one
with new force in the pauses of the night that the Chaldeans were a
desert-bred people. It is hard to escape the sense of mastery as the
stars move in the wide clear heavens to risings and settings unobscured.

They look large and near and palpitant; as if they moved on some stately service not needful to declare. Wheeling to their stations in the sky, they make the poor world-fret of no account. Of no account you who lie out there watching, nor the lean coyote that stands off in the scrub from you and howls and howls.

WATER TRAILS OF THE CERISO

By the end of the dry season the water trails of the Ceriso are worn to a white ribbon in the leaning grass, spread out faint and fanwise toward the homes of gopher and ground rat and squirrel. But however faint to man-sight, they are sufficiently plain to the furred and feathered folk who travel them. Getting down to the eye level of rat and squirrel kind, one perceives what might easily be wide and winding roads to us if they occurred in thick plantations of trees three times the height of a man. It needs but a slender thread of barrenness to make a mouse trail in the forest of the sod. To the little people the water trails are as country roads, with scents as signboards.

It seems that man-height is the least fortunate of all heights from which to study trails. It is better to go up the front of some tall hill, say the spur of Black Mountain, looking back and down across the hollow of the Ceriso. Strange how long the soil keeps the impression of any continuous treading, even after grass has overgrown it. Twenty years since, a brief heyday of mining at Black Mountain made a stage road across the Ceriso, yet the parallel lines that are the wheel traces show from the height dark and well defined. Afoot in the Ceriso one looks in vain for any sign of it. So all the paths that wild creatures use going down to the Lone Tree Spring are mapped out whitely from this level, which is also the level of the hawks.

There is little water in the Ceriso at the best of times, and that little brackish and smelling vilely, but by a lone juniper where the rim of the Ceriso breaks away to the lower country, there is a perpetual rill of fresh sweet drink in the midst of lush grass and watercress. In the dry season there is no water else for a man's long journey of a day. East to the foot of Black Mountain, and north and south without counting, are the burrows of small rodents, rat and squirrel kind. Under the sage are the shallow forms of the jackrabbits, and in the dry banks of washes, and among the strewn fragments of black rock, lairs of bobcat, fox, and coyote.

The coyote is your true water-witch, one who snuffs and paws, snuffs and paws again at the smallest spot of moisture-scented earth until he has freed the blind water from the soil. Many water-holes are no more than this detected by the lean hobo of the hills in localities where not even an Indian would look for it. It is the opinion of many wise and busy people that the hill-folk pass the ten-month interval between the end and renewal of winter rains, with no drink; but your true idler, with days and nights to spend beside the water trails, will not subscribe to it. The trails begin, as I said, very far back in the Ceriso, faintly, and converge in one span broad, white, hard-trodden way in the gully of the spring. And why trails if there are no travelers in that direction?

I have yet to find the land not scarred by the thin, far roadways of rabbits and what not of furry folks that run in them. Venture to look for some seldom-touched water-hole, and so long as the trails run with your general direction make sure you are right, but if they begin to cross yours at never so slight an angle, to converge toward a point left or right of your objective, no matter what the maps say, or your memory, trust them; they *know*.

It is very still in the Ceriso by day, so that were it not for the evidence of those white beaten ways, it might be the desert it looks. The sun is hot in the dry season, and the days are filled with the glare of it. Now and again some unseen coyote signals his pack in a long-drawn, dolorous whine that comes from no determinate point, but nothing stirs much before mid-afternoon. It is a sign when there begin to be hawks skimming above the sage that the little people are going about their business.

We have fallen on a very careless usage, speaking of wild creatures as if they were bound by some such limitation as hampers clockwork. When we say of one and another, they are night prowlers, it is perhaps true only as the things they feed upon are more easily come by in the dark, and they know well how to adjust themselves to conditions wherein food is more plentiful by day. And their accustomed performance is very much a matter of keen eye, keener scent, quick ear, and a better memory of sights and sounds than man dares boast. Watch a coyote come out of his lair and cast about in his mind where he will go for his daily killing. You cannot very well tell what decides him, but very easily that he has decided. He trots or breaks into short gallops, with very perceptible pauses to look up and about at landmarks, alters his tack a little, looking forward and back to steer his proper course. I am persuaded that the coyotes in my valley, which is narrow and beset with steep, sharp hills, in long passages steer by the pinnacles of the sky-line, going with head cocked to one side to keep to the left or right of such and such a promontory.

I have trailed a coyote often, going across country, perhaps to where some slant-winged scavenger hanging in the air signaled prospect of a dinner, and found his track such as a man, a very intelligent man accustomed to a hill country, and a little cautious, would make to the same point. Here a detour to avoid a stretch of too little cover, there a pause on the rim of a gully to pick the better way,—and it is usually the best way,—and making his point with the greatest economy of effort. Since the time of Seyavi the deer have shifted their feeding ground across the valley at the beginning of deep snows, by way of the Black Rock, fording the river at Charley's Butte, and making straight for the mouth of the cañon that is the easiest going to the winter pastures on Waban. So they still cross, though whatever trail they had has been long broken by ploughed ground; but from the mouth of Tinpah Creek, where the deer come out of the Sierras, it is easily seen that the creek, the point of Black Rock, and Charley's Butte are in line with the wide bulk of shade that is the foot of Waban Pass. And along with this the deer have learned that Charley's Butte is almost the only possible ford, and all the shortest crossing of the valley. It seems that the wild creatures have learned all that is important to their way of life except the changes of the moon. I have seen some prowling fox or coyote, surprised by its sudden rising from behind the mountain wall, slink in its increasing glow, watch it furtively from the cover of near-by brush, unprepared and half uncertain of its identity until it rode clear of the peaks, and finally make off with all the air of one caught napping by an ancient joke. The moon in its wanderings must be a sort of exasperation to cunning beasts, likely to spoil by untimely risings some fore-planned mischief. But to take the trail again; the coyotes that are astir in the Ceriso of late afternoons, harrying the rabbits from their shallow forms, and the hawks that sweep and swing above them, are not there from any mechanical promptings of instinct, but because they know of old experience that the small fry are about to take to seed gathering and the water trails. The rabbits begin it, taking the trail with long, light leaps, one eye and ear cocked to the hills from whence a coyote might descend upon them at any moment. Rabbits are a foolish people. They do not fight except with their own kind, nor use their paws except for feet, and appear to have no reason for existence but to furnish meals for meat-eaters. In flight they seem to rebound from the earth of their own elasticity, but keep a sober pace going to the spring. It is the young watercress that tempts them and the pleasures of society, for they seldom drink. Even in localities where there are flowing streams they seem to prefer the moisture that collects on herbage, and after rains may be seen rising on their haunches to drink delicately the clear drops caught in the tops of the young sage. But drink they must, as I have often seen them mornings and evenings at the rill that goes by my door. Wait long enough at the Lone Tree Spring and sooner or later they will all come in. But here their matings are accomplished, and though they are fearful of so little as a cloud shadow or blown leaf, they contrive to have some playful hours. At the spring the bobcat drops down upon them from the black rock, and the red fox picks them up returning in the dark. By day the hawk and eagle overshadow them, and the coyote has all times and seasons for his own.

Cattle, when there are any in the Ceriso, drink morning and evening, spending the night on the warm last lighted slopes of neighboring hills, stirring with the peep o' day. In these half wild spotted steers the habits of an earlier lineage persist. It must be long since they have made beds for themselves, but before lying down they turn themselves round and round as dogs do. They choose bare and stony ground, exposed fronts of westward facing hills, and lie down in companies. Usually by the end of the summer the cattle have been driven or gone of their own choosing to the mountain meadows. One year a maverick yearling, strayed or overlooked by the vaqueros, kept on until the season's end, and so betrayed another visitor to the spring that else I might have missed. On a certain morning the half-eaten carcass lay at the foot of the black rock, and in moist earth by the rill of the spring, the foot-pads of a cougar, puma, mountain lion, or whatever the beast is rightly called. The kill must have been made early in the evening, for it appeared that the cougar had been twice to the spring; and since the meat-eater drinks little until he has eaten, he must have fed and drunk, and after an interval of lying up in the black rock, had eaten and drunk again. There was no knowing how far he had come, but if he came again the second night he found that the coyotes had left him very little of his kill.

Nobody ventures to say how infrequently and at what hour the small fry visit the spring. There are such numbers of them that if each came once between the last of spring and the first of winter rains, there would still be water trails. I have seen badgers drinking about the hour when the light takes on the yellow tinge it has from coming slantwise through the hills. They find out shallow places, and are loath to wet their feet. Rats and chipmunks have been observed visiting the spring as late as nine o'clock mornings. The larger spermophiles that live near the spring and keep awake to work all day, come and go at no particular hour, drinking sparingly. At long intervals on half-lighted days, meadow and field mice steal delicately along the trail. These visitors are all too small to be watched carefully at night, but for evidence of their frequent coming there are the trails that may be traced miles out among the crisping grasses. On rare nights, in the places where no grass grows between the shrubs, and the sand silvers whitely to the moon, one sees them whisking to and fro on innumerable errands of seed gathering, but the chief witnesses of their presence near the spring are the elf owls. Those burrow-haunting, speckled fluffs of greediness begin a twilight flitting toward the spring, feeding as they go on grasshoppers, lizards, and small, swift creatures, diving into burrows to catch field mice asleep, battling with chipmunks at their own doors, and getting down in great numbers toward the lone juniper. Now owls do not love water greatly on its own account. Not to my knowledge have I caught one drinking or bathing, though on night wanderings across the mesa they flit up from under the horse's feet along stream borders. Their presence near the spring in great numbers would indicate the presence of the things they feed upon. All night the rustle and soft hooting keeps on in the neighborhood of the spring, with seldom small shrieks of mortal agony. It is clear day before they have all gotten back to their particular hummocks, and if one follows cautiously, not to frighten them into some near-by burrow, it is possible to trail them far up the slope.

The crested quail that troop in the Ceriso are the happiest frequenters of the water trails. There is no furtiveness about their morning drink. About the time the burrowers and all that feed upon them are addressing themselves to sleep, great flocks pour down the trails with that peculiar melting motion of moving quail, twittering, shoving, and shouldering. They splatter into the shallows, drink daintily, shake out small showers over their perfect coats, and melt away again into the scrub, preening and pranking, with soft contented noises.

After the quail, sparrows and ground-inhabiting birds bathe with the utmost frankness and a great deal of splutter; and here in the heart of noon hawks resort, sitting panting, with wings aslant, and a truce to all hostilities because of the heat. One summer there came a road-runner up from the lower valley, peeking and prying, and he had never any patience with the water baths of the sparrows. His own ablutions were performed in the clean, hopeful dust of the chaparral; and whenever he happened on their morning splatterings, he would depress his glossy crest, slant his shining tail to the level of his body, until he looked most like some bright venomous snake, daunting them with shrill abuse and feint of battle. Then suddenly he would go tilting and balancing down the gully in fine disdain, only to return in a day or two to make sure the foolish bodies were still at it.

Out on the Ceriso about five miles, and wholly out of sight of it, near where the immemorial foot trail goes up from Saline Flat toward Black Mountain, is a water sign worth turning out of the trail to see. It is a laid circle of stones large enough not to be disturbed by any ordinary hap, with an opening flanked by two parallel rows of similar stones, between which were an arrow placed, touching the opposite rim of the circle, it would point as the crow flies to the spring. It is the old, indubitable water mark of the Shoshones. One still finds it in the desert ranges in Salt Wells and Mesquite valleys, and along the slopes of Waban. On the other side of Ceriso, where the black rock begins, about a mile from the spring, is the work of an older, forgotten people. The rock hereabout is all volcanic, fracturing with a crystalline whitish surface, but weathered outside to furnace blackness. Around the spring, where must have been a gathering place of the tribes, it is scored over with strange pictures and symbols that have no meaning to the Indians of the present day; but out where the rock begins, there is carved into the white heart of it a pointing arrow over the symbol for distance and a circle full of wavy lines reading thus: "In this direction three [units of measurement unknown] is a spring of sweet water; look for it."

THE SCAVENGERS

Fifty-seven buzzards, one on each of fifty-seven fence posts at the rancho El Tejon, on a mirage-breeding September morning, sat solemnly while the white tilted travelers' vans lumbered down the Canada de los Uvas. After three hours they had only clapped their wings, or exchanged posts. The season's end in the vast dim valley of the San Joaquin is palpitatingly hot, and the air breathes like cotton wool. Through it all the buzzards sit on the fences and low hummocks, with wings spread fanwise for air. There is no end to them, and they smell to heaven. Their heads droop, and all their communication is a rare, horrid croak.

The increase of wild creatures is in proportion to the things they feed upon: the more carrion the more buzzards. The end of the third successive dry year bred them beyond belief. The first year quail mated sparingly; the second year the wild oats matured no seed; the third, cattle died in their tracks with their heads towards the stopped watercourses. And that year the scavengers were as black as the plague all across the mesa and up the treeless, tumbled hills. On clear days they betook themselves to the upper air, where they hung motionless for hours. That year there were vultures among them, distinguished by the white patches under the wings. All their offensiveness notwithstanding, they have a stately flight. They must also have what pass for good qualities among themselves, for they are social, not to say clannish.

It is a very squalid tragedy,—that of the dying brutes and the scavenger birds. Death by starvation is slow. The heavy-headed, rack-boned cattle totter in the fruitless trails; they stand for long, patient intervals; they lie down and do not rise. There is fear in their eyes when they are first stricken, but afterward only intolerable weariness. I suppose the dumb creatures know, nearly as much of death as do their betters, who have only the more imagination. Their even-breathing submission after the first agony is their tribute to its inevitableness. It needs a nice discrimination to say which of the basket-ribbed cattle is likest to afford the next meal, but the scavengers make few mistakes. One stoops to the quarry and the flock follows.

Cattle once down may be days in dying, They stretch out their necks along the ground, and roll up their slow eyes at longer intervals. The buzzards have all the time, and no beak is dropped or talon struck until the breath is wholly passed. It is doubtless the economy of nature to have the scavengers by to clean up the carrion, but a wolf at the throat would be a shorter agony than the long stalking and sometime perchings of these loathsome watchers. Suppose now it were a man in this long-drawn, hungrily spied upon distress! When Timmie O'Shea was lost on Armogossa Flats for three days without water, Long Tom Basset found him, not by any trail, but by making straight away for the points where he saw buzzards stooping. He could hear the beat of their wings, Tom said, and trod on their shadows, but O'Shea was past recalling what he thought about things after the second day. My friend Ewan told me, among other things, when he came back from San Juan Hill, that not all the carnage of battle turned his bowels as the sight of slant black wings rising flockwise before the burial squad.

There are three kinds of noises buzzards make,—it is impossible to call them notes,—raucous and elemental. There is a short croak of alarm, and the same syllable in a modified tone to serve all the purposes of ordinary conversation. The old birds make a kind of throaty chuckling to their young, but if they have any love song I have not heard it. The young yawp in the nest a little, with more breath than noise. It is seldom one finds a buzzard's nest, seldom that grown-ups find a nest of any sort; it is only children to whom these things happen by right. But by making a business of it one may come upon them in wide, quiet cañons, or on the lookouts of lonely, table-topped mountains, three or four together, in the tops of stubby trees or on rotten cliffs well open to the sky.

It is probable that the buzzard is gregarious, but it seems unlikely from the small number of young noted at any time that every female incubates each year. The young birds are easily distinguished by their size when feeding, and high up in air by the worn primaries of the older birds. It is when the young go out of the nest on their first foraging that the parents, full of a crass and simple pride, make their indescribable chucklings of gobbling, gluttonous delight. The little ones would be amusing as they tug and tussle, if one could forget what it is they feed upon.

One never comes any nearer to the vulture's nest or nestlings than hearsay. They keep to the southerly Sierras, and are bold enough, it seems, to do killing on their own account when no carrion is at hand. They dog the shepherd from camp to camp, the hunter home from the hill, and will even carry away offal from under his hand.

The vulture merits respect for his bigness and for his bandit airs, but he is a sombre bird, with none of the buzzard's frank satisfaction in his offensiveness.

The least objectionable of the inland scavengers is the raven, frequenter of the desert ranges, the same called locally "carrion crow." He is handsomer and has such an air. He is nice in his habits and is said to have likable traits. A tame one in a Shoshone camp was the butt of much sport and enjoyed it. He could all but talk and was another with the children, but an arrant thief. The raven will eat most things that come his way,—eggs and young of ground-nesting birds, seeds even, lizards and grasshoppers, which he catches cleverly; and whatever he is about, let a coyote trot never so softly by, the raven flaps up and after; for whatever the coyote can pull down or nose out is meat also for the carrion crow.

And never a coyote comes out of his lair for killing, in the country of the carrion crows, but looks up first to see where they may be gathering. It is a sufficient occupation for a windy morning, on the lineless, level mesa, to watch the pair of them eying each other furtively, with a tolerable assumption of unconcern, but no doubt with a certain amount of good understanding about it. Once at Red Rock, in a year of green pasture, which is a bad time for the scavengers, we saw two buzzards, five ravens, and a coyote feeding on the same carrion, and only the coyote seemed ashamed of the company.

Probably we never fully credit the interdependence of wild creatures, and their cognizance of the affairs of their own kind. When the five coyotes that range the Tejon from Pasteria to Tunawai planned a relay race to bring down an antelope strayed from the band, beside myself to watch, an eagle swung down from Mt. Pinos, buzzards materialized out of invisible ether, and hawks came trooping like small boys to a street fight. Rabbits sat up in the chaparral and cocked their ears, feeling themselves quite safe for the once as the hunt swung near them. Nothing happens in the deep wood that the blue jays are not all agog to tell. The hawk follows the badger, the coyote the carrion crow, and from their aerial stations the buzzards watch each other. What would be worth knowing is how much of their neighbor's affairs the new generations learn for themselves, and how much they are taught of their elders.

So wide is the range of the scavengers that it is never safe to say, eyewitness to the contrary, that there are few or many in such a place. Where the carrion is, there will the buzzards be gathered together, and in three days' journey you will not sight another one. The way up from Mojave to Red Butte is all desertness, affording no pasture and scarcely a rill of water. In a year of little rain in the south, flocks and herds were driven to the number of thousands along this road to the perennial pastures of the high ranges. It is a long, slow trail, ankle deep in bitter dust that gets up in the slow wind and moves along the backs of the crawling cattle. In the worst of times one in three will pine and fall out by the way. In the defiles of Red Rock, the sheep piled up a stinking lane; it was the sun smiting by day. To these shambles came buzzards, vultures, and coyotes from all the country round, so that on the Tejon, the Ceriso, and the Little Antelope there were not scavengers enough to keep the country clean. All that summer the dead mummified in the open or dropped slowly back to earth in the quagmires of the bitter springs. Meanwhile from Red Rock to Coyote Holes, and from Coyote Holes to Haiwai the scavengers gorged and gorged.

The coyote is not a scavenger by choice, preferring his own kill, but being on the whole a lazy dog, is apt to fall into carrion eating because it is easier. The red fox and bobcat, a little pressed by hunger, will eat of any other animal's kill, but will not ordinarily touch what dies of itself, and are exceedingly shy of food that has been manhandled.

Very clean and handsome, quite belying his relationship in appearance, is Clark's crow, that scavenger and plunderer of mountain camps. It is permissible to call him by his common name, "Camp Robber:" he has earned it. Not content with refuse, he pecks open meal sacks, filches whole potatoes, is a gormand for bacon, drills holes in packing cases, and is daunted by nothing short of tin. All the while he does not neglect to vituperate the chipmunks and sparrows that whisk off crumbs of comfort from under the camper's feet. The Camp Robber's gray coat, black and white barred wings, and slender bill, with certain tricks of perching, accuse him of attempts to pass himself off among woodpeckers; but his behavior is all crow. He frequents the higher pine belts, and has a noisy strident call like a jay's, and how clean he and the frisk-tailed chipmunks keep the camp! No crumb or paring or bit of eggshell goes amiss.

High as the camp may be, so it is not above timber-line, it is not too high for the coyote, the bobcat, or the wolf. It is the complaint of the ordinary camper that the woods are too still, depleted of wild life. But what dead body of wild thing, or neglected game untouched by its kind, do you find? And put out offal away from camp over night, and look next day at the foot tracks where it lay.

Man is a great blunderer going about in the woods, and there is no other except the bear makes so much noise. Being so well warned beforehand, it is a very stupid animal, or a very bold one, that cannot keep safely hid. The cunningest hunter is hunted in turn, and what he leaves of his kill is meat for some other. That is the economy of nature, but with it all there is not sufficient account taken of the works of man. There is no scavenger that eats tin cans, and no wild thing leaves a like disfigurement on the forest floor.

THE POCKET HUNTER

I remember very well when I first met him. Walking in the evening glow to spy the marriages of the white gilias, I sniffed the unmistakable odor of burning sage. It is a smell that carries far and indicates usually the nearness of a campoodie, but on the level mesa nothing taller showed than Diana's sage. Over the tops of it, beginning to dusk under a young white moon, trailed a wavering ghost of smoke, and at the end of it I came upon the Pocket Hunter making a dry camp in the friendly scrub. He sat tailorwise in the sand, with his coffee-pot on the coals, his supper ready to hand in the frying pan, and himself in a mood for talk. His pack burros in hobbles strayed off to hunt for a wetter mouthful than the sage afforded, and gave him no concern.

We came upon him often after that, threading the windy passes, or by water-holes in the desert hills, and got to know much of his way of life. He was a small, bowed man, with a face and manner and speech of no character at all, as if he had that faculty of small hunted things of taking on the protective color of his surroundings. His clothes were of no fashion that I could remember, except that they bore liberal markings of pot black, and he had a curious fashion of going about with his mouth open, which gave him a vacant look until you came near enough to perceive him busy about an endless hummed, wordless tune. He traveled far and took a long time to it, but the simplicity of his kitchen arrangements was elemental. A pot for beans, a coffee-pot, a frying-pan, a tin to mix bread in—he fed the burros in this when there was need—with these he had been half round our western world and back. He explained to me very early in our acquaintance what was good to take to the hills for food: nothing sticky, for that "dirtied the pots;" nothing with "juice" to it, for that would not pack to advantage; and nothing likely to ferment. He used no gun, but he would set snares by the water-holes for quail and doves, and in the trout country he carried a line. Burros he kept, one or two according to his pack, for this chief excellence, that they would eat potato parings and firewood. He had owned a horse in the foothill country, but when he came to the desert with no forage but mesquite, he found himself under the necessity of picking the beans from the briers, a labor that drove him to the use of pack animals to whom thorns were a relish.

I suppose no man becomes a pocket hunter by first intention. He must be born with the faculty, and along comes the occasion, like the tap on the test tube that induces crystallization. My friend had been several things of no moment until he struck a thousand-dollar pocket in the Lee District and came into his vocation. A pocket, you must know, is a small body of rich ore occurring by itself, or in a vein of poorer stuff. Nearly every mineral ledge contains such, if only one has the luck to hit upon them without too much labor. The sensible thing for a man to do who has found a good pocket is to buy himself into business and keep away from the hills. The logical thing is to set out looking for another one. My friend the Pocket Hunter had been looking twenty years. His working outfit was a shovel, a pick, a gold pan which he kept cleaner than his plate, and a pocket magnifier. When he came to a watercourse he would pan out the gravel of its bed for "colors," and under the glass determine if they had come from far or near, and so spying he would work up the stream until he found where the drift of the gold-bearing outcrop fanned out into the creek; then up the side of the cañon till he came to the proper vein. I think he said the best indication of small pockets was an iron stain, but I could never get the run of miner's talk enough to feel instructed for pocket hunting. He had another method in the waterless hills, where he would work in and out of blind gullies and all windings of the manifold strata that appeared not to have cooled since they had been heaved up. His itinerary began with the east slope of the Sierras of the Snows, where that range swings across to meet the coast hills, and all up that slope to the Truckee River country, where the long cold forbade his progress north. Then he worked back down one or another of the nearly parallel ranges that lie out desertward, and so down to the sink of the Mojave River, burrowing to oblivion in the sand,—a big mysterious land, a lonely, inhospitable land, beautiful, terrible. But he came to no harm in it; the land tolerated him as it might a gopher or a badger. Of all its inhabitants it has the least concern for man.

There are many strange sorts of humans bred in a mining country, each sort despising the queernesses of the other, but of them all I found the Pocket Hunter most acceptable for his clean, companionable talk.

There was more color to his reminiscences than the faded sandy old miners "kyote-ing," that is, tunneling like a coyote (kyote in the vernacular) in the core of a lonesome hill. Such a one has found, perhaps, a body of tolerable ore in a poor lead,—remember that I can never be depended on to get the terms right,— and followed it into the heart of country rock to no profit, hoping, burrowing, and hoping. These men go harmlessly mad in time, believing themselves just behind the wall of fortune—most likable and simple men, for whom it is well to do any kindly thing that occurs to you except lend them money. I have known "grub stakers" too, those persuasive sinners to whom you make allowances of flour and pork and coffee in consideration of the ledges they are about to find; but none of these proved so much worth while as the Pocket Hunter. He wanted nothing of you and maintained a cheerful preference for his own way of life. It was an excellent way if you had the constitution for it. The Pocket Hunter had gotten to that point where he knew no bad weather, and all places were equally happy so long as they were out of doors. I do not know just how long it takes to become saturated with the elements so that one takes no account of them. Myself can never get past the glow and exhilaration of a storm, the wrestle of long dust-heavy winds, the play of live thunder on the rocks, nor past the keen fret of fatigue when the storm outlasts physical endurance. But prospectors and Indians get a kind of a weather shell that remains on the body until death.

The Pocket Hunter had seen destruction by the violence of nature and the violence of men, and felt himself in the grip of an All-wisdom that killed men or spared them as seemed for their good; but of death by sickness he knew nothing except that he believed he should never suffer it. He had been in Grape-vine Cañon the year of storms that changed the whole front of the mountain. All day he had come down under the wing of the storm, hoping to win past it, but finding it traveling with him until night. It kept on after that, he supposed, a steady downpour, but could not with certainty say, being securely deep in sleep. But the weather instinct does not sleep. In the night the heavens behind the hill dissolved in rain, and the roar of the storm was borne in and mixed with his dreaming, so that it moved him, still asleep, to get up and out of the path of it. What finally woke him was the crash of pine logs as they went down before the unbridled flood, and the swirl of foam that lashed him where he clung in the tangle of scrub while the wall of water went by. It went on against the cabin of Bill Gerry and laid Bill stripped and broken on a sand bar at the mouth of the Grape-vine, seven miles away. There, when the sun was up and the wrath of the rain spent, the Pocket Hunter found and buried him; but he never laid his own escape at any door but the unintelligible favor of the Powers. The journeyings of the Pocket Hunter led him often into that mysterious country beyond Hot Creek where a hidden force works mischief, mole-like, under the crust of the earth. Whatever agency is at work in that neighborhood, and it is popularly supposed to be the devil, it changes means and direction without time or season. It creeps up whole hillsides with insidious heat, unguessed until one notes the pine woods dying at the top, and having scorched out a good block of timber returns to steam and spout in caked, forgotten crevices of years before. It will break up sometimes blue-hot and bubbling, in the midst of a clear creek, or make a sucking, scalding quicksand at the ford. These outbreaks had the kind of morbid interest for the Pocket Hunter that a house of unsavory reputation has in a respectable neighborhood, but I always found the accounts he brought me more interesting than his explanations, which were compounded of fag ends of miner's talk and superstition. He was a perfect gossip of the woods, this Pocket Hunter, and when I could get him away from "leads" and "strikes" and "contacts," full of fascinating small talk about the ebb and flood of creeks, the piñon crop on Black Mountain, and the wolves of Mesquite Valley. I suppose he never knew how much he depended for the necessary sense of home and companionship on the beasts and trees, meeting and finding them in their wonted places,—the bear that used to come down Pine Creek in the spring, pawing out trout from the shelters of sod banks, the juniper at Lone Tree Spring, and the quail at Paddy Jack's.

There is a place on Waban, south of White Mountain, where flat, wind-tilted cedars make low tents and coves of shade and shelter, where the wild sheep winter in the snow. Woodcutters and prospectors had brought me word of that, but the Pocket Hunter was accessory to the fact. About the opening of winter, when one looks for sudden big storms, he had attempted a crossing by the nearest path, beginning the ascent at noon. It grew cold, the snow came on thick and blinding, and wiped out the trail in a white smudge; the storm drift blew in and cut off landmarks, the early dark obscured the rising drifts. According to the Pocket Hunter's account, he knew where he was, but couldn't exactly say. Three days before he had been in the west arm of Death Valley on a short water allowance, ankle-deep in shifty sand; now he was on the rise of Waban, knee-deep in sodden snow, and in both cases he did the only allowable thing—he walked on. That is the only thing to do in a snowstorm in any case. It might have been the creature instinct, which in his way of life had room to grow, that led him to the cedar shelter; at any rate he found it about four hours after dark, and heard the heavy breathing of the flock. He said that if he thought at all at this juncture he must have thought that he had stumbled on a storm-belated shepherd with his silly sheep; but in fact he took no note of anything but the warmth of packed fleeces, and snuggled in between them dead with sleep. If the flock stirred in the night he stirred drowsily to keep close and let the storm go by. That was all until morning woke him shining on a white world. Then the very soul of him shook to see the wild sheep of God stand up about him, nodding their great horns beneath the cedar roof, looking out on the wonder of the snow. They had moved a little away from him with the coming of the light, but paid him no more heed. The light broadened and the white pavilions of the snow swam in the heavenly blueness of the sea from which they rose. The cloud drift scattered and broke billowing in the cañons. The leader stamped lightly on the litter to put the flock in motion, suddenly they took the drifts in those long light leaps that are nearest to flight, down and away on the slopes of Waban. Think of that to happen to a Pocket Hunter! But though he had fallen on many a wished-for hap, he was curiously inapt at getting the truth about beasts in general. He believed in the venom of toads, and charms for snake bites, and— for this I could never forgive him—had all the miner's prejudices against my friend the coyote. Thief, sneak, and son of a thief were the friendliest words he had for this little gray dog of the wilderness.

Of course with so much seeking he came occasionally upon pockets of more or less value, otherwise he could not have kept up his way of life; but he had as much luck in missing great ledges as in finding small ones. He had been all over the Tonopah country, and brought away float without happening upon anything that gave promise of what that district was to become in a few years. He claimed to have chipped bits off the very outcrop of the California Rand, without finding it worth while to bring away, but none of these things put him out of countenance.

It was once in roving weather, when we found him shifting pack on a steep trail, that I observed certain of his belongings done up in green canvas bags, the veritable "green bag" of English novels. It seemed so incongruous a reminder in this untenanted West that I dropped down beside the trail overlooking the vast dim valley, to hear about the green canvas. He had gotten it, he said, in London years before, and that was the first I had known of his having been abroad. It was after one of his "big strikes" that he had made the Grand Tour, and had brought nothing away from it but the green canvas bags, which he conceived would fit his needs, and an ambition. This last was nothing less than to strike it rich and set himself up among the eminently bourgeois of London. It seemed that the situation of the wealthy English middle class, with just enough gentility above to aspire to, and sufficient smaller fry to bully and patronize, appealed to his imagination, though of course he did not put it so crudely as that. It was no news to me then, two or three years after, to learn that he had taken ten thousand dollars from an abandoned claim, just the sort of luck to have pleased him, and gone to London to spend it. The land seemed not to miss him any more than it had minded him, but I missed him and could not forget the trick of expecting him in least likely situations. Therefore it was with a pricking sense of the familiar that I followed a twilight trail of smoke, a year or two later, to the swale of a dripping spring, and came upon a man by the fire with a coffee-pot and frying-pan. I was not surprised to find it was the Pocket Hunter. No man can be stronger than his destiny.

SHOSHONE LAND

It is true I have been in Shoshone Land, but before that, long before, I had seen it through the eyes of Winnenap' in a rosy mist of reminiscence, and must always see it with a sense of intimacy in the light that never was. Sitting on the golden slope at the campoodie, looking across the Bitter Lake to the purple tops of Mutarango, the medicine-man drew up its happy places one by one, like little blessed islands in a sea of talk. For he was born a Shoshone, was Winnenap'; and though his name, his wife, his children, and his tribal relations were of the Paiutes, his thoughts turned homesickly toward Shoshone Land. Once a Shoshone always a Shoshone. Winnenap' lived gingerly among the Paiutes and in his heart despised them. But he could speak a tolerable English when he would, and he always would if it were of Shoshone Land.

He had come into the keeping of the Paiutes as a hostage for the long peace which the authority of the whites made interminable, and, though there was now no order in the tribe, nor any power that could have lawfully restrained him, kept on in the old usage, to save his honor and the word of his vanished kin. He had seen his children's children in the borders of the Paiutes, but loved best his own miles of sand and rainbow-painted hills. Professedly he had not seen them since the beginning of his hostage; but every year about the end of the rains and before the strength of the sun had come upon us from the south, the medicine-man went apart on the mountains to gather herbs, and when he came again I knew by the new fortitude of his countenance and the new color of his reminiscences that he had been alone and unspied upon in Shoshone Land.

To reach that country from the campoodie, one goes south and south, within hearing of the lip-lip-lapping of the great tideless lake, and south by east over a high rolling district, miles and miles of sage and nothing else. So one comes to the country of the painted hills,—old red cones of craters, wasteful beds of mineral earths, hot, acrid springs, and steam jets issuing from a leprous soil. After the hills the black rock, after the craters the spewed lava, ash strewn, of incredible thickness, and full of sharp, winding rifts. There are picture writings carved deep in the face of the cliffs to mark the way for those who do not know it. On the very edge of the black rock the earth falls away in a wide sweeping hollow, which is Shoshone Land.

South the land rises in very blue hills, blue because thickly wooded with ceanothus and manzanita, the haunt of deer and the border of the Shoshones. Eastward the land goes very far by broken ranges, narrow valleys of pure desertness, and huge mesas uplifted to the sky-line, east and east, and no man knows the end of it.

It is the country of the bighorn, the wapiti, and the wolf, nesting place of buzzards, land of cloud-nourished trees and wild things that live without drink. Above all, it is the land of the creosote and the mesquite. The mesquite is God's best thought in all this desertness. It grows in the open, is thorny, stocky, close grown, and iron-rooted. Long winds move in the draughty valleys, blown sand fills and fills about the lower branches, piling pyramidal dunes, from the top of which the mesquite twigs flourish greenly. Fifteen or twenty feet under the drift, where it seems no rain could penetrate, the main trunk grows, attaining often a yard's thickness, resistant as oak. In Shoshone Land one digs for large timber; that is in the southerly, sandy exposures. Higher on the table-topped ranges low trees of juniper and piñon stand each apart, rounded and spreading heaps of greenness. Between them, but each to itself in smooth clear spaces, tufts of tall feathered grass.

This is the sense of the desert hills, that there is room enough and time enough. Trees grow to consummate domes; every plant has its perfect work. Noxious weeds such as come up thickly in crowded fields do not flourish in the free spaces. Live long enough with an Indian, and he or the wild things will show you a use for everything that grows in these borders.

The manner of the country makes the usage of life there, and the land will not be lived in except in its own fashion. The Shoshones live like their trees, with great spaces between, and in pairs and in family groups they set up wattled huts by the infrequent springs. More wickiups than two make a very great number. Their shelters are lightly built, for they travel much and far, following where deer feed and seeds ripen, but they are not more lonely than other creatures that inhabit there.

The year's round is somewhat in this fashion. After the piñon harvest the clans foregather on a warm southward slope for the annual adjustment of tribal difficulties and the medicine dance, for marriage and mourning and vengeance, and the exchange of serviceable information; if, for example, the deer have shifted their feeding ground, if the wild sheep have come back to Waban, or certain springs run full or dry. Here the Shoshones winter flockwise, weaving baskets and hunting big game driven down from the country of the deep snow. And this brief intercourse is all the use they have of their kind, for now there are no wars, and many of their ancient crafts have fallen into disuse. The solitariness of the life breeds in the men, as in the plants, a certain well-roundedness and sufficiency to its own ends. Any Shoshone family has in itself the man-seed, power to multiply and replenish, potentialities for food and clothing and shelter, for healing and beautifying.

When the rain is over and gone they are stirred by the instinct of those that journeyed eastward from Eden, and go up each with his mate and young brood, like birds to old nesting places. The beginning of spring in Shoshone Land—oh the soft wonder of it!—is a mistiness as of incense smoke, a veil of greenness over the whitish stubby shrubs, a web of color on the silver sanded soil. No counting covers the multitude of rayed blossoms that break suddenly underfoot in the brief season of the winter rains, with silky furred or prickly viscid foliage, or no foliage at all. They are morning and evening bloomers chiefly, and strong seeders. Years of scant rains they lie shut and safe in the winnowed sands, so that some species appear to be extinct. Years of long storms they break so thickly into bloom that no horse treads without crushing them. These years the gullies of the hills are rank with fern and a great tangle of climbing vines.

Just as the mesa twilights have their vocal note in the love call of the burrowing owl, so the desert spring is voiced by the mourning doves. Welcome and sweet they sound in the smoky mornings before breeding time, and where they frequent in any great numbers water is confidently looked for. Still by the springs one finds the cunning brush shelters from which the Shoshones shot arrows at them when the doves came to drink.

Now as to these same Shoshones there are some who claim that they have no right to the name, which belongs to a more northerly tribe; but that is the word they will be called by, and there is no greater offense than to call an Indian out of his name. According to their traditions and all proper evidence, they were a great people occupying far north and east of their present bounds, driven thence by the Paiutes. Between the two tribes is the residuum of old hostilities.

Winnenap', whose memory ran to the time when the boundary of the Paiute country was a dead-line to Shoshones, told me once how himself and another lad, in an unforgotten spring, discovered a nesting place of buzzards a bit of a way beyond the borders. And they two burned to rob those nests. Oh, for no purpose at all except as boys rob nests immemorially, for the fun of it, to have and handle and show to other lads as an exceeding treasure, and afterwards discard. So, not quite meaning to, but breathless with daring, they crept up a gully, across a sage brush flat and through a waste of boulders, to the rugged pines where their sharp eyes had made out the buzzards settling.

The medicine-man told me, always with a quaking relish at this point, that while they, grown bold by success, were still in the tree, they sighted a Paiute hunting party crossing between them and their own land. That was mid-morning, and all day on into the dark the boys crept and crawled and slid, from boulder to bush, and bush to boulder, in cactus scrub and on naked sand, always in a sweat of fear, until the dust caked in the nostrils and the breath sobbed in the body, around and away many a mile until they came to their own land again. And all the time Winnenap' carried those buzzard's eggs in the slack of his single buckskin garment! Young Shoshones are like young quail, knowing without teaching about feeding and hiding, and learning what civilized children never learn, to be still and to keep on being still, at the first hint of danger or strangeness.

As for food, that appears to be chiefly a matter of being willing. Desert Indians all eat chuck-wallas, big black and white lizards that have delicate white flesh savored like chicken. Both the Shoshones and the coyotes are fond of the flesh of *Gopherus agassizii*, the turtle that by feeding on buds, going without drink, and burrowing in the sand through the winter, contrives to live a known period of twenty-five years. It seems that most seeds are foodful in the arid regions, most berries edible, and many shrubs good for firewood with the sap in them. The mesquite bean, whether the screw or straight pod, pounded to a meal, boiled to a kind of mush, and dried in cakes, sulphur-colored and needing an axe to cut it, is an excellent food for long journeys. Fermented in water with wild honey and the honeycomb, it makes a pleasant, mildly intoxicating drink.

Next to spring, the best time to visit Shoshone Land is when the deer-star hangs low and white like a torch over the morning hills. Go up past Winnedumah and down Saline and up again to the rim of Mesquite Valley. Take no tent, but if you will, have an Indian build you a wickiup, willows planted in a circle, drawn over to an arch, and bound cunningly with withes, all the leaves on, and chinks to count the stars through. But there was never any but Winnenap' who could tell and make it worth telling about Shoshone Land.

And Winnenap' will not any more. He died, as do most medicine-men of the Paiutes.

Where the lot falls when the campoodie chooses a medicine-man there it rests. It is an honor a man seldom seeks but must wear, an honor with a condition. When three patients die under his ministrations, the medicine-man must yield his life and his office. Wounds do not count; broken bones and bullet holes the Indian can understand, but measles, pneumonia, and smallpox are witchcraft. Winnenap' was medicine-man for fifteen years. Besides considerable skill in healing herbs, he used his prerogatives cunningly. It is permitted the medicine-man to decline the case when the patient has had treatment from any other, say the white doctor, whom many of the younger generation consult. Or, if before having seen the patient, he can definitely refer his disorder to some supernatural cause wholly out of the medicine-man's jurisdiction, say to the spite of an evil spirit going about in the form of a coyote, and states the case convincingly, he may avoid the penalty. But this must not be pushed too far. All else failing, he can hide. Winnenap' did this the time of the measles epidemic. Returning from his yearly herb gathering, he heard of it at Black Rock, and turning aside, he was not to be found, nor did he return to his own place until the disease had spent itself, and half the children of the campoodie were in their shallow graves with beads sprinkled over them.

It is possible the tale of Winnenap''s patients had not been strictly kept. There had not been a medicine-man killed in the valley for twelve years, and for that the perpetrators had been severely punished by the whites. The winter of the Big Snow an epidemic of pneumonia carried off the Indians with scarcely a warning; from the lake northward to the lava flats they died in the sweat-houses, and under the hands of the medicine-men. Even the drugs of the white physician had no power. After two weeks of this plague the Paiutes drew to council to consider the remissness of their medicine-men. They were sore with grief and afraid for themselves; as a result of the council, one in every campoodie was sentenced to the ancient penalty. But schooling and native shrewdness had raised up in the younger men an unfaith in old usages, so judgment halted between sentence and execution. At Three Pines the government teacher brought out influential whites to threaten and cajole the stubborn tribes. At Tunawai the conservatives sent into Nevada for that pacific old humbug, Johnson Sides, most notable of Paiute orators, to harangue his people. Citizens of the towns turned out with food and comforts, and so after a season the trouble passed.

But here at Maverick there was no school, no oratory, and no alleviation. One third of the campoodie died, and the rest killed the medicine-men. Winnenap expected it, and for days walked and sat a little apart from his family that he might meet it as became a Shoshone, no doubt suffering the agony of dread deferred. When finally three men came and sat at his fire without greeting he knew his time.

He turned a little from them, dropped his chin upon his knees, and looked out over Shoshone Land, breathing evenly. The women went into the wickiup and covered their heads with their blankets.

So much has the Indian lost of savageness by merely desisting from killing, that the executioners braved themselves to their work by drinking and a show of quarrelsomeness. In the end a sharp hatchet-stroke discharged the duty of the campoodie. Afterward his women buried him, and a warm wind coming out of the south, the force of the disease was broken, and even they acquiesced in the wisdom of the tribe. That summer they told me all except the names of the Three.

Since it appears that we make our own heaven here, no doubt we shall have a hand in the heaven of hereafter; and I know what Winnenap's will be like: worth going to if one has leave to live in it according to his liking. It will be tawny gold underfoot, walled up with jacinth and jasper, ribbed with chalcedony, and yet no hymn-book heaven, but the free air and free spaces of Shoshone Land.

JIMVILLE—A BRET HARTE TOWN

When Mr. Harte found himself with a fresh palette and his particular local color fading from the West, he did what he considered the only safe thing, and carried his young impression away to be worked out untroubled by any newer fact. He should have gone to Jimville. There he would have found cast up on the ore-ribbed hills the bleached timbers of more tales, and better ones.

You could not think of Jimville as anything more than a survival, like the herb-eating, bony-cased old tortoise that pokes cheerfully about those borders some thousands of years beyond his proper epoch.

Not that Jimville is old, but it has an atmosphere favorable to the type of a half century back, if not "forty-niners," of that breed. It is said of Jimville that getting away from it is such a piece of work that it encourages permanence in the population; the fact is that most have been drawn there by some real likeness or liking. Not however that I would deny the difficulty of getting into or out of that cove of reminder, I who have made the journey so many times at great pains of a poor body. Any way you go at it, Jimville is about three days from anywhere in particular. North or south, after the railroad there is a stage journey of such interminable monotony as induces forgetfulness of all previous states of existence.

The road to Jimville is the happy hunting ground of old stage-coaches bought up from superseded routes the West over, rocking, lumbering, wide vehicles far gone in the odor of romance, coaches that Vasquez has held up, from whose high seats express messengers have shot or been shot as their luck held. This is to comfort you when the driver stops to rummage for wire to mend a failing bolt. There is enough of this sort of thing to quite prepare you to believe what the driver insists, namely, that all that country and Jimville are held together by wire.

First on the way to Jimville you cross a lonely open land, with a hint in the sky of things going on under the horizon, a palpitant, white, hot land where the wheels gird at the sand and the midday heaven shuts it in breathlessly like a tent. So in still weather; and when the wind blows there is occupation enough for the passengers, shifting seats to hold down the windward side of the wagging coach. This is a mere trifle. The Jimville stage is built for five passengers, but when you have seven, with four trunks, several parcels, three sacks of grain, the mail and express, you begin to understand that proverb about the road which has been reported to you. In time you learn to engage the high seat beside the driver, where you get good air and the best company. Beyond the desert rise the lava flats, scoriae strewn; sharp-cutting walls of narrow cañons; league-wide, frozen puddles of black rock, intolerable and forbidding. Beyond the lava the mouths that spewed it out, ragged-lipped, ruined craters shouldering to the cloud-line, mostly of red earth, as red as a red heifer. These have some comforting of shrubs and grass. You get the very spirit of the meaning of that country when you see Little Pete feeding his sheep in the red, choked maw of an old vent,—a kind of silly pastoral gentleness that glazes over an elemental violence. Beyond the craters rise worn, auriferous hills of a quiet sort, tumbled together; a valley full of mists; whitish green scrub; and bright, small, panting lizards; then Jimville.

The town looks to have spilled out of Squaw Gulch, and that, in fact, is the sequence of its growth. It began around the Bully Boy and Theresa group of mines midway up Squaw Gulch, spreading down to the smelter at the mouth of the ravine. The freight wagons dumped their loads as near to the mill as the slope allowed, and Jimville grew in between. Above the Gulch begins a pine wood with sparsely grown thickets of lilac, azalea, and odorous blossoming shrubs.

Squaw Gulch is a very sharp, steep, ragged-walled ravine, and that part of Jimville which is built in it has only one street,—in summer paved with bone-white cobbles, in the wet months a frothy yellow flood. All between the ore dumps and solitary small cabins, pieced out with tin cans and packing cases, run footpaths drawing down to the Silver Dollar saloon. When Jimville was having the time of its life the Silver Dollar had those same coins let into the bar top for a border, but the proprietor pried them out when the glory departed. There are three hundred inhabitants in Jimville and four bars, though you are not to argue anything from that.

Hear now how Jimville came by its name. Jim Calkins discovered the Bully Boy, Jim Baker located the Theresa. When Jim Jenkins opened an eating-house in his tent he chalked up on the flap, "Best meals in Jimville, $1.00," and the name stuck.

There was more human interest in the origin of Squaw Gulch, though it tickled no humor. It was Dimmick's squaw from Aurora way. If Dimmick had been anything except New Englander he would have called her a mahala, but that would not have bettered his behavior. Dimmick made a strike, went East, and the squaw who had been to him as his wife took to drink. That was the bald way of stating it in the Aurora country. The milk of human kindness, like some wine, must not be uncorked too much in speech lest it lose savor. This is what they did. The woman would have returned to her own people, being far gone with child, but the drink worked her bane. By the river of this ravine her pains overtook her. There Jim Calkins, prospecting, found her dying with a three days' babe nozzling at her breast. Jim heartened her for the end, buried her, and walked back to Poso, eighteen miles, the child poking in the folds of his denim shirt with small mewing noises, and won support for it from the rough-handed folks of that place. Then he came back to Squaw Gulch, so named from that day, and discovered the Bully Boy. Jim humbly regarded this piece of luck as interposed for his reward, and I for one believed him. If it had been in mediaeval times you would have had a legend or a ballad. Bret Harte would have given you a tale. You see in me a mere recorder, for I know what is best for you; you shall blow out this bubble from your own breath.

You could never get into any proper relation to Jimville unless you could slough off and swallow your acquired prejudices as a lizard does his skin. Once wanting some womanly attentions, the stage-driver assured me I might have them at the Nine-Mile House from the lady barkeeper. The phrase tickled all my after-dinner-coffee sense of humor into an anticipation of Poker Flat. The stage-driver proved himself really right, though you are not to suppose from this that Jimville had no conventions and no caste. They work out these things in the personal equation largely. Almost every latitude of behavior is allowed a good fellow, one no liar, a free spender, and a backer of his friends' quarrels. You are respected in as much ground as you can shoot over, in as many pretensions as you can make good.

That probably explains Mr. Fanshawe, the gentlemanly faro dealer of those parts, built for the role of Oakhurst, going white-shirted and frock-coated in a community of overalls; and persuading you that whatever shifts and tricks of the game were laid to his deal, he could not practice them on a person of your penetration. But he does. By his own account and the evidence of his manners he had been bred for a clergyman, and he certainly has gifts for the part. You find him always in possession of your point of view, and with an evident though not obtrusive desire to stand well with you. For an account of his killings, for his way with women and the way of women with him, I refer you to Brown of Calaveras and some others of that stripe. His improprieties had a certain sanction of long standing not accorded to the gay ladies who wore Mr. Fanshawe's favors. There were perhaps too many of them. On the whole, the point of the moral distinctions of Jimville appears to be a point of honor, with an absence of humorous appreciation that strangers mistake for dullness. At Jimville they see behavior as history and judge it by facts, untroubled by invention and the dramatic sense. You glimpse a crude equity in their dealings with Wilkins, who had shot a man at Lone Tree, fairly, in an open quarrel. Rumor of it reached Jimville before Wilkins rested there in flight. I saw Wilkins, all Jimville saw him; in fact, he came into the Silver Dollar when we were holding a church fair and bought a pink silk pincushion. I have often wondered what became of it. Some of us shook hands with him, not because we did not know, but because we had not been officially notified, and there were those present who knew how it was themselves. When the sheriff arrived Wilkins had moved on, and Jimville organized a posse and brought him back, because the sheriff was a Jimville man and we had to stand by him.

I said we had the church fair at the Silver Dollar. We had most things there, dances, town meetings, and the kinetoscope exhibition of the Passion Play. The Silver Dollar had been built when the borders of Jimville spread from Minton to the red hill the Defiance twisted through. "Side-Winder" Smith scrubbed the floor for us and moved the bar to the back room. The fair was designed for the support of the circuit rider who preached to the few that would hear, and buried us all in turn. He was the symbol of Jimville's respectability, although he was of a sect that held dancing among the cardinal sins. The management took no chances on offending the minister; at 11.30 they tendered him the receipts of the evening in the chairman's hat, as a delicate intimation that the fair was closed. The company filed out of the front door and around to the back. Then the dance began formally with no feelings hurt. These were the sort of courtesies, common enough in Jimville, that brought tears of delicate inner laughter.

There were others besides Mr. Fanshawe who had walked out of Mr. Harte's demesne to Jimville and wore names that smacked of the soil,—"Alkali Bill," "Pike" Wilson, "Three Finger," and "Mono Jim;" fierce, shy, profane, sun-dried derelicts of the windy hills, who each owned, or had owned, a mine and was wishful to own one again. They laid up on the worn benches of the Silver Dollar or the Same Old Luck like beached vessels, and their talk ran on endlessly of "strike" and "contact" and "mother lode," and worked around to fights and hold-ups, villainy, haunts, and the hoodoo of the Minietta, told austerely without imagination.

Do not suppose I am going to repeat it all; you who want these things written up from the point of view of people who do not do them every day would get no savor in their speech.

Says Three Finger, relating the history of the Mariposa, "I took it off'n Tom Beatty, cheap, after his brother Bill was shot."

Says Jim Jenkins, "What was the matter of him?"

"Who? Bill? Abe Johnson shot him; he was fooling around Johnson's wife, an' Tom sold me the mine dirt cheap."

"Why didn't he work it himself?"

"Him? Oh, he was laying for Abe and calculated to have to leave the country pretty quick."

"Huh!" says Jim Jenkins, and the tale flows smoothly on.

Yearly the spring fret floats the loose population of Jimville out into the desolate waste hot lands, guiding by the peaks and a few rarely touched water-holes, always, always with the golden hope. They develop prospects and grow rich, develop others and grow poor but never embittered. Say the hills, It is all one, there is gold enough, time enough, and men enough to come after you. And at Jimville they understand the language of the hills.

Jimville does not know a great deal about the crust of the earth, it prefers a "hunch." That is an intimation from the gods that if you go over a brown back of the hills, by a dripping spring, up Coso way, you will find what is worth while. I have never heard that the failure of any particular hunch disproved the principle. Somehow the rawness of the land favors the sense of personal relation to the supernatural. There is not much intervention of crops, cities, clothes, and manners between you and the organizing forces to cut off communication. All this begets in Jimville a state that passes explanation unless you will accept an explanation that passes belief. Along with killing and drunkenness, coveting of women, charity, simplicity, there is a certain indifference, blankness, emptiness if you will, of all vaporings, no bubbling of the pot,—it wants the German to coin a word for that,—no bread-envy, no brother-fervor. Western writers have not sensed it yet; they smack the savor of lawlessness too much upon their tongues, but you have these to witness it is not mean-spiritedness. It is pure Greek in that it represents the courage to sheer off what is not worth while. Beyond that it endures without sniveling, renounces without self-pity, fears no death, rates itself not too great in the scheme of things; so do beasts, so did St. Jerome in the desert, so also in the elder day did gods. Life, its performance, cessation, is no new thing to gape and wonder at.

Here you have the repose of the perfectly accepted instinct which includes passion and death in its perquisites. I suppose that the end of all our hammering and yawping will be something like the point of view of Jimville. The only difference will be in the decorations.

MY NEIGHBOR'S FIELD

It is one of those places God must have meant for a field from all time, lying very level at the foot of the slope that crowds up against Kearsarge, falling slightly toward the town. North and south it is fenced by low old glacial ridges, boulder strewn and untenable. Eastward it butts on orchard closes and the village gardens, brimming over into them by wild brier and creeping grass. The village street, with its double row of unlike houses, breaks off abruptly at the edge of the field in a footpath that goes up the streamside, beyond it, to the source of waters.

The field is not greatly esteemed of the town, not being put to the plough nor affording firewood, but breeding all manner of wild seeds that go down in the irrigating ditches to come up as weeds in the gardens and grass plots. But when I had no more than seen it in the charm of its spring smiling, I knew I should have no peace until I had bought ground and built me a house beside it, with a little wicket to go in and out at all hours, as afterward came about.

Edswick, Roeder, Connor, and Ruffin owned the field before it fell to my neighbor. But before that the Paiutes, mesne lords of the soil, made a campoodie by the rill of Pine Creek; and after, contesting the soil with them, cattle-men, who found its foodful pastures greatly to their advantage; and bands of blethering flocks shepherded by wild, hairy men of little speech, who attested their rights to the feeding ground with their long staves upon each other's skulls. Edswick homesteaded the field about the time the wild tide of mining life was roaring and rioting up Kearsarge, and where the village now stands built a stone hut, with loopholes to make good his claim against cattle-men or Indians. But Edswick died and Roeder became master of the field. Roeder owned cattle on a thousand hills, and made it a recruiting ground for his bellowing herds before beginning the long drive to market across a shifty desert. He kept the field fifteen years, and afterward falling into difficulties, put it out as security against certain sums. Connor, who held the securities, was cleverer than Roeder and not so busy. The money fell due the winter of the Big Snow, when all the trails were forty feet under drifts, and Roeder was away in San Francisco selling his cattle. At the set time Connor took the law by the forelock and was adjudged possession of the field. Eighteen days later Roeder arrived on snowshoes, both feet frozen, and the money in his pack. In the long suit at law ensuing, the field fell to Ruffin, that clever one-armed lawyer with the tongue to wile a bird out of the bush, Connor's counsel, and was sold by him to my neighbor, whom from envying his possession I call Naboth.

Curiously, all this human occupancy of greed and mischief left no mark on the field, but the Indians did, and the unthinking sheep. Round its corners children pick up chipped arrow points of obsidian, scattered through it are kitchen middens and pits of old sweat-houses. By the south corner, where the campoodie stood, is a single shrub of "hoopee" (*Lycium Andersonii*), maintaining itself hardly among alien shrubs, and near by, three low rakish trees of hackberry, so far from home that no prying of mine has been able to find another in any cañon east or west. But the berries of both were food for the Paiutes, eagerly sought and traded for as far south as Shoshone Land. By the fork of the creek where the shepherds camp is a single clump of mesquite of the variety called "screw bean." The seed must have shaken there from some sheep's coat, for this is not the habitat of mesquite, and except for other single shrubs at sheep camps, none grows freely for a hundred and fifty miles south or east.

Naboth has put a fence about the best of the field, but neither the Indians nor the shepherds can quite forego it. They make camp and build their wattled huts about the borders of it, and no doubt they have some sense of home in its familiar aspect.

As I have said, it is a low-lying field, between the mesa and the town, with no hillocks in it, but a gentle swale where the waste water of the creek goes down to certain farms, and the hackberry-trees, of which the tallest might be three times the height of a man, are the tallest things in it. A mile up from the water gate that turns the creek into supply pipes for the town, begins a row of long-leaved pines, threading the watercourse to the foot of Kearsarge. These are the pines that puzzle the local botanist, not easily determined, and unrelated to other conifers of the Sierra slope; the same pines of which the Indians relate a legend mixed of brotherliness and the retribution of God. Once the pines possessed the field, as the worn stumps of them along the streamside show, and it would seem their secret purpose to regain their old footing. Now and then some seedling escapes the devastating sheep a rod or two down-stream. Since I came to live by the field one of these has tiptoed above the gully of the creek, beckoning the procession from the hills, as if in fact they would make back toward that skyward-pointing finger of granite on the opposite range, from which, according to the legend, when they were bad Indians and it a great chief, they ran away. This year the summer floods brought the round, brown, fruitful cones to my very door, and I look, if I live long enough, to see them come up greenly in my neighbor's field.

It is interesting to watch this retaking of old ground by the wild plants, banished by human use. Since Naboth drew his fence about the field and restricted it to a few wild-eyed steers, halting between the hills and the shambles, many old habitués of the field have come back to their haunts. The willow and brown birch, long ago cut off by the Indians for wattles, have come back to the streamside, slender and virginal in their spring greenness, and leaving long stretches of the brown water open to the sky. In stony places where no grass grows, wild olives sprawl; close-twigged, blue-gray patches in winter, more translucent greenish gold in spring than any aureole. Along with willow and birch and brier, the clematis, that shyest plant of water borders, slips down season by season to within a hundred yards of the village street. Convinced after three years that it would come no nearer, we spent time fruitlessly pulling up roots to plant in the garden. All this while, when no coaxing or care prevailed upon any transplanted slip to grow, one was coming up silently outside the fence near the wicket, coiling so secretly in the rabbit-brush that its presence was never suspected until it flowered delicately along its twining length. The horehound comes through the fence and under it, shouldering the pickets off the railings; the brier rose mines under the horehound; and no care, though I own I am not a close weeder, keeps the small pale moons of the primrose from rising to the night moth under my apple-trees. The first summer in the new place, a clump of cypripediums came up by the irrigating ditch at the bottom of the lawn. But the clematis will not come inside, nor the wild almond.

I have forgotten to find out, though I meant to, whether the wild almond grew in that country where Moses kept the flocks of his father-in-law, but if so one can account for the burning bush. It comes upon one with a flame-burst as of revelation; little hard red buds on leafless twigs, swelling unnoticeably, then one, two, or three strong suns, and from tip to tip one soft fiery glow, whispering with bees as a singing flame. A twig of finger size will be furred to the thickness of one's wrist by pink five-petaled bloom, so close that only the blunt-faced wild bees find their way in it. In this latitude late frosts cut off the hope of fruit too often for the wild almond to multiply greatly, but the spiny, tap-rooted shrubs are resistant to most plant evils.

It is not easy always to be attentive to the maturing of wild fruit. Plants are so unobtrusive in their material processes, and always at the significant moment some other bloom has reached its perfect hour. One can never fix the precise moment when the rosy tint the field has from the wild almond passes into the inspiring blue of lupines. One notices here and there a spike of bloom, and a day later the whole field royal and ruffling lightly to the wind. Part of the charm of the lupine is the continual stir of its plumes to airs not suspected otherwhere. Go and stand by any crown of bloom and the tall stalks do but rock a little as for drowsiness, but look off across the field, and on the stillest days there is always a trepidation in the purple patches.

From midsummer until frost the prevailing note of the field is clear gold, passing into the rusty tone of bigelovia going into a decline, a succession of color schemes more admirably managed than the transformation scene at the theatre. Under my window a colony of cleome made a soft web of bloom that drew me every morning for a long still time; and one day I discovered that I was looking into a rare fretwork of fawn and straw colored twigs from which both bloom and leaf had gone, and I could not say if it had been for a matter of weeks or days. The time to plant cucumbers and set out cabbages may be set down in the almanac, but never seed-time nor blossom in Naboth's field.

Certain winged and mailed denizens of the field seem to reach their heyday along with the plants they most affect. In June the leaning towers of the white milkweed are jeweled over with red and gold beetles, climbing dizzily. This is that milkweed from whose stems the Indians flayed fibre to make snares for small game, but what use the beetles put it to except for a displaying ground for their gay coats, I could never discover. The white butterfly crop comes on with the bigelovia bloom, and on warm mornings makes an airy twinkling all across the field. In September young linnets grow out of the rabbit-brush in the night. All the nests discoverable in the neighboring orchards will not account for the numbers of them. Somewhere, by the same secret process by which the field matures a million more seeds than it needs, it is maturing red-hooded linnets for their devouring. All the purlieus of bigelovia and artemisia are noisy with them for a month. Suddenly as they come as suddenly go the fly-by-nights, that pitch and toss on dusky barred wings above the field of summer twilights. Never one of these nighthawks will you see after linnet time, though the hurtle of their wings makes a pleasant sound across the dusk in their season.

For two summers a great red-tailed hawk has visited the field every afternoon between three and four o'clock, swooping and soaring with the airs of a gentleman adventurer. What he finds there is chiefly conjectured, so secretive are the little people of Naboth's field. Only when leaves fall and the light is low and slant, one sees the long clean flanks of the jackrabbits, leaping like small deer, and of late afternoons little cotton-tails scamper in the runways. But the most one sees of the burrowers, gophers, and mice is the fresh earthwork of their newly opened doors, or the pitiful small shreds the butcher-bird hangs on spiny shrubs.

It is a still field, this of my neighbor's, though so busy, and admirably compounded for variety and pleasantness,—a little sand, a little loam, a grassy plot, a stony rise or two, a full brown stream, a little touch of humanness, a footpath trodden out by moccasins. Naboth expects to make town lots of it and his fortune in one and the same day; but when I take the trail to talk with old Seyavi at the campoodie, it occurs to me that though the field may serve a good turn in those days it will hardly be happier. No, certainly not happier.

THE MESA TRAIL

The mesa trail begins in the campoodie at the corner of Naboth's field, though one may drop into it from the wood road toward the cañon, or from any of the cattle paths that go up along the streamside; a clean, pale, smooth-trodden way between spiny shrubs, comfortably wide for a horse or an Indian. It begins, I say, at the campoodie, and goes on toward the twilight hills and the borders of Shoshone Land. It strikes diagonally across the foot of the hill-slope from the field until it reaches the larkspur level, and holds south along the front of Oppapago, having the high ranges to the right and the foothills and the great Bitter Lake below it on the left. The mesa holds very level here, cut across at intervals by the deep washes of dwindling streams, and its treeless spaces uncramp the soul.

Mesa trails were meant to be traveled on horseback, at the jigging coyote trot that only western-bred horses learn successfully. A foot-pace carries one too slowly past the units in a decorative scheme that is on a scale with the country round for bigness. It takes days' journeys to give a note of variety to the country of the social shrubs. These chiefly clothe the benches and eastern foot-slopes of the Sierras,—great spreads of artemisia, *coleogyne*, and spinosa, suffering no other woody stemmed thing in their purlieus; this by election apparently, with no elbowing; and the several shrubs have each their clientèle of flowering herbs. It would be worth knowing how much the devastating sheep have had to do with driving the tender plants to the shelter of the prickle-bushes. It might have begun earlier, in the time Seyavi of the campoodie tells of, when antelope ran on the mesa like sheep for numbers, but scarcely any foot-high herb rears itself except from the midst of some stout twigged shrub; larkspur in the *coleogyne*, and for every spinosa the purpling coils of phacelia. In the shrub shelter, in the season, flock the little stemless things whose blossom time is as short as a marriage song. The larkspurs make the best showing, being tall and sweet, swaying a little above the shrubbery, scattering pollen dust which Navajo brides gather to fill their marriage baskets. This were an easier task than to find two of them of a shade. Larkspurs in the botany are blue, but if you were to slip rein to the stub of some black sage and set about proving it you would be still at it by the hour when the white gilias set their pale disks to the westering sun. This is the gilia the children call "evening snow," and it is no use trying to improve on children's names for wild flowers.

From the height of a horse you look down to clean spaces in a shifty yellow soil, bare to the eye as a newly sanded floor. Then as soon as ever the hill shadows begin to swell out from the sidelong ranges, come little flakes of whiteness fluttering at the edge of the sand. By dusk there are tiny drifts in the lee of every strong shrub, rosy-tipped corollas as riotous in the sliding mesa wind as if they were real flakes shaken out of a cloud, not sprung from the ground on wiry three-inch stems. They keep awake all night, and all the air is heavy and musky sweet because of them.

Farther south on the trail there will be poppies meeting ankle deep, and singly, peacock-painted bubbles of calochortus blown out at the tops of tall stems. But before the season is in tune for the gayer blossoms the best display of color is in the lupin wash. There is always a lupin wash somewhere on a mesa trail,—a broad, shallow, cobble-paved sink of vanished waters, where the hummocks of *Lupinus ornatus* run a delicate gamut from silvery green of spring to silvery white of winter foliage. They look in fullest leaf, except for color, most like the huddled huts of the campoodie, and the largest of them might be a man's length in diameter. In their season, which is after the gilias are at their best, and before the larkspurs are ripe for pollen gathering, every terminal whorl of the lupin sends up its blossom stalk, not holding any constant blue, but paling and purpling to guide the friendly bee to virginal honey sips, or away from the perfected and depleted flower. The length of the blossom stalk conforms to the rounded contour of the plant, and of these there will be a million moving indescribably in the airy current that flows down the swale of the wash.

There is always a little wind on the mesa, a sliding current of cooler air going down the face of the mountain of its own momentum, but not to disturb the silence of great space. Passing the wide mouths of cañons, one gets the effect of whatever is doing in them, openly or behind a screen of cloud,—thunder of falls, wind in the pine leaves, or rush and roar of rain. The rumor of tumult grows and dies in passing, as from open doors gaping on a village street, but does not impinge on the effect of solitariness. In quiet weather mesa days have no parallel for stillness, but the night silence breaks into certain mellow or poignant notes. Late afternoons the burrowing owls may be seen blinking at the doors of their hummocks with perhaps four or five elfish nestlings arow, and by twilight begin a soft *whoo-oo-ing*, rounder, sweeter, more incessant in mating time. It is not possible to disassociate the call of the burrowing owl from the late slant light of the mesa. If the fine vibrations which are the golden-violet glow of spring twilights were to tremble into sound, it would be just that mellow double note breaking along the blossom-tops. While the glow holds one sees the thistle-down flights and pouncings after prey, and on into the dark hears their soft *pus-ssh!* clearing out of the trail ahead. Maybe the pin-point shriek of field mouse or kangaroo rat that pricks the wakeful pauses of the night is extorted by these mellow-voiced plunderers, though it is just as like to be the work of the red fox on his twenty-mile constitutional.

Both the red fox and the coyote are free of the night hours, and both killers for the pure love of slaughter. The fox is no great talker, but the coyote goes garrulously through the dark in twenty keys at once, gossip, warning, and abuse. They are light treaders, the split-feet, so that the solitary camper sees their eyes about him in the dark sometimes, and hears the soft intake of breath when no leaf has stirred and no twig snapped underfoot. The coyote is your real lord of the mesa, and so he makes sure you are armed with no long black instrument to spit your teeth into his vitals at a thousand yards, is both bold and curious. Not so bold, however, as the badger and not so much of a curmudgeon. This short-legged meat-eater loves half lights and lowering days, has no friends, no enemies, and disowns his offspring. Very likely if he knew how hawk and crow dog him for dinners, he would resent it. But the badger is not very well contrived for looking up or far to either side. Dull afternoons he may be met nosing a trail hot-foot to the home of ground rat or squirrel, and is with difficulty persuaded to give the right of way. The badger is a pot-hunter and no sportsman. Once at the hill, he dives for the central chamber, his sharp-clawed, splayey feet splashing up the sand like a bather in the surf. He is a swift trailer, but not so swift or secretive but some small sailing hawk or lazy crow, perhaps one or two of each, has spied upon him and come drifting down the wind to the killing.

No burrower is so unwise as not to have several exits from his dwelling under protecting shrubs. When the badger goes down, as many of the furry people as are not caught napping come up by the back doors, and the hawks make short work of them. I suspect that the crows get nothing but the gratification of curiosity and the pickings of some secret store of seeds unearthed by the badger. Once the excavation begins they walk about expectantly, but the little gray hawks beat slow circles about the doors of exit, and are wiser in their generation, though they do not look it.

There are always solitary hawks sailing above the mesa, and where some blue tower of silence lifts out of the neighboring range, an eagle hanging dizzily, and always buzzards high up in the thin, translucent air making a merry-go-round. Between the coyote and the birds of carrion the mesa is kept clear of miserable dead.

The wind, too, is a besom over the treeless spaces, whisking new sand over the litter of the scant-leaved shrubs, and the little doorways of the burrowers are as trim as city fronts. It takes man to leave unsightly scars on the face of the earth. Here on the mesa the abandoned campoodies of the Paiutes are spots of desolation long after the wattles of the huts have warped in the brush heaps. The campoodies are near the watercourses, but never in the swale of the stream. The Paiute seeks rising ground, depending on air and sun for purification of his dwelling, and when it becomes wholly untenable, moves.

A campoodie at noontime, when there is no smoke rising and no stir of life, resembles nothing so much as a collection of prodigious wasps' nests. The huts are squat and brown and chimneyless, facing east, and the inhabitants have the faculty of quail for making themselves scarce in the underbrush at the approach of strangers. But they are really not often at home during midday, only the blind and incompetent left to keep the camp. These are working hours, and all across the mesa one sees the women whisking seeds of *chia* into their spoon-shaped baskets, these emptied again into the huge conical carriers, supported on the shoulders by a leather band about the forehead.

Mornings and late afternoons one meets the men singly and afoot on unguessable errands, or riding shaggy, browbeaten ponies, with game slung across the saddle-bows. This might be deer or even antelope, rabbits, or, very far south towards Shoshone Land, lizards.

There are myriads of lizards on the mesa, little gray darts, or larger salmon-sided ones that may be found swallowing their skins in the safety of a prickle-bush in early spring. Now and then a palm's breadth of the trail gathers itself together and scurries off with a little rustle under the brush, to resolve itself into sand again. This is pure witchcraft. If you succeed in catching it in transit, it loses its power and becomes a flat, horned, toad-like creature, horrid looking and harmless, of the color of the soil; and the curio dealer will give you two bits for it, to stuff.

Men have their season on the mesa as much as plants and four-footed things, and one is not like to meet them out of their time. For example, at the time of *rodeos*, which is perhaps April, one meets free riding vaqueros who need no trails and can find cattle where to the layman no cattle exist. As early as February bands of sheep work up from the south to the high Sierra pastures. It appears that shepherds have not changed more than sheep in the process of time. The shy hairy men who herd the tractile flocks might be, except for some added clothing, the very brethren of David. Of necessity they are hardy, simple livers, superstitious, fearful, given to seeing visions, and almost without speech. It needs the bustle of shearings and copious libations of sour, weak wine to restore the human faculty. Petite Pete, who works a circuit up from the Ceriso to Red Butte and around by way of Salt Flats, passes year by year on the mesa trail, his thick hairy chest thrown open to all weathers, twirling his long staff, and dealing brotherly with his dogs, who are possibly as intelligent, certainly handsomer.

A flock's journey is seven miles, ten if pasture fails, in a windless blur of dust, feeding as it goes, and resting at noons. Such hours Pete weaves a little screen of twigs between his head and the sun—the rest of him is as impervious as one of his own sheep—and sleeps while his dogs have the flocks upon their consciences. At night, wherever he may be, there Pete camps, and fortunate the trail-weary traveler who falls in with him. When the fire kindles and savory meat seethes in the pot, when there is a drowsy blether from the flock, and far down the mesa the twilight twinkle of shepherd fires, when there is a hint of blossom underfoot and a heavenly whiteness on the hills, one harks back without effort to Judaea and the Nativity. But one feels by day anything but good will to note the shorn shrubs and cropped blossom-tops. So many seasons' effort, so many suns and rains to make a pound of wool! And then there is the loss of ground-inhabiting birds that must fail from the mesa when few herbs ripen seed.

Out West, the west of the mesas and the unpatented hills, there is more sky than any place in the world. It does not sit flatly on the rim of earth, but begins somewhere out in the space in which the earth is poised, hollows more, and is full of clean winey winds. There are some odors, too, that get into the blood. There is the spring smell of sage that is the warning that sap is beginning to work in a soil that looks to have none of the juices of life in it; it is the sort of smell that sets one thinking what a long furrow the plough would turn up here, the sort of smell that is the beginning of new leafage, is best at the plant's best, and leaves a pungent trail where wild cattle crop. There is the smell of sage at sundown, burning sage from campoodies and sheep camps, that travels on the thin blue wraiths of smoke; the kind of smell that gets into the hair and garments, is not much liked except upon long acquaintance, and every Paiute and shepherd smells of it indubitably. There is the palpable smell of the bitter dust that comes up from the alkali flats at the end of the dry seasons, and the smell of rain from the wide-mouthed cañons.

And last the smell of the salt grass country, which is the beginning of other things that are the end of the mesa trail.

THE BASKET MAKER

"A Man," says Seyavi of the campoodie, "must have a woman, but a woman who has a child will do very well."

That was perhaps why, when she lost her mate in the dying struggle of his race, she never took another, but set her wit to fend for herself and her young son. No doubt she was often put to it in the beginning to find food for them both. The Paiutes had made their last stand at the border of the Bitter Lake; battle-driven they died in its waters, and the land filled with cattle-men and adventurers for gold: this while Seyavi and the boy lay up in the caverns of the Black Rock and ate tule roots and fresh-water clams that they dug out of the slough bottoms with their toes.

In the interim, while the tribes swallowed their defeat, and before the rumor of war died out, they must have come very near to the bare core of things. That was the time Seyavi learned the sufficiency of mother wit, and how much more easily one can do without a man than might at first be supposed.

To understand the fashion of any life, one must know the land it is lived in and the procession of the year. This valley is a narrow one, a mere trough between hills, a draught for storms, hardly a crow's flight from the sharp Sierras of the Snows to the curled, red and ochre, uncomforted, bare ribs of Waban. Midway of the groove runs a burrowing, dull river, nearly a hundred miles from where it cuts the lava flats of the north to its widening in a thick, tideless pool of a lake. Hereabouts the ranges have no foothills, but rise up steeply from the bench lands above the river. Down from the Sierras, for the east ranges have almost no rain, pour glancing white floods toward the lowest land, and all beside them lie the campoodies, brown wattled brush heaps, looking east.

In the river are mussels, and reeds that have edible white roots, and in the soddy meadows tubers of joint grass; all these at their best in the spring. On the slope the summer growth affords seeds; up the steep the one-leafed pines, an oily nut. That was really all they could depend upon, and that only at the mercy of the little gods of frost and rain. For the rest it was cunning against cunning, caution against skill, against quacking hordes of wild-fowl in the tulares, against pronghorn and bighorn and deer. You can guess, however, that all this warring of rifles and bowstrings, this influx of overlording whites, had made game wilder and hunters fearful of being hunted. You can surmise also, for it was a crude time and the land was raw, that the women became in turn the game of the conquerors.

There used to be in the Little Antelope a she dog, stray or outcast, that had a litter in some forsaken lair, and ranged and foraged for them, slinking savage and afraid, remembering and mistrusting humankind, wistful, lean, and sufficient for her young. I have thought Seyavi might have had days like that, and have had perfect leave to think, since she will not talk of it. Paiutes have the art of reducing life to its lowest ebb and yet saving it alive on grasshoppers, lizards, and strange herbs; and that time must have left no shift untried.

It lasted long enough for Seyavi to have evolved the philosophy of life which I have set down at the beginning. She had gone beyond learning to do for her son, and learned to believe it worth while.

In our kind of society, when a woman ceases to alter the fashion of her hair, you guess that she has passed the crisis of her experience. If she goes on crimping and uncrimping with the changing mode, it is safe to suppose she has never come up against anything too big for her. The Indian woman gets nearly the same personal note in the pattern of her baskets. Not that she doe's not make all kinds, carriers, water-bottles, and cradles,—these are kitchen ware,— but her works of art are all of the same piece. Seyavi made flaring, flat-bottomed bowls, cooking pots really, when cooking was done by dropping hot stones into water-tight food baskets, and for decoration a design in colored bark of the procession of plumed crests of the valley quail. In this pattern she had made cooking pots in the golden spring of her wedding year, when the quail went up two and two to their resting places about the foot of Oppapago. In this fashion she made them when, after pillage, it was possible to reinstate the housewifely crafts. Quail ran then in the Black Rock by hundreds,—so you will still find them in fortunate years,—and in the famine time the women cut their long hair to make snares when the flocks came morning and evening to the springs.

Seyavi made baskets for love and sold them for money, in a generation that preferred iron pots for utility. Every Indian woman is an artist,—sees, feels, creates, but does not philosophize about her processes. Seyavi's bowls are wonders of technical precision, inside and out, the palm finds no fault with them, but the subtlest appeal is in the sense that warns us of humanness in the way the design spreads into the flare of the bowl. There used to be an Indian woman at Olancha who made bottle-neck trinket baskets in the rattlesnake pattern, and could accommodate the design to the swelling bowl and flat shoulder of the basket without sensible disproportion, and so cleverly that you might own one a year without thinking how it was done; but Seyavi's baskets had a touch beyond cleverness. The weaver and the warp lived next to the earth and were saturated with the same elements. Twice a year, in the time of white butterflies and again when young quail ran neck and neck in the chaparral, Seyavi cut willows for basketry by the creek where it wound toward the river against the sun and sucking winds. It never quite reached the river except in far-between times of summer flood, but it always tried, and the willows encouraged it as much as they could. You nearly always found them a little farther down than the trickle of eager water. The Paiute fashion of counting time appeals to me more than any other calendar. They have no stamp of heathen gods nor great ones, nor any succession of moons as have red men of the East and North, but count forward and back by the progress of the season; the time of *taboose*, before the trout begin to leap, the end of the piñon harvest, about the beginning of deep snows. So they get nearer the sense of the season, which runs early or late according as the rains are forward or delayed. But whenever Seyavi cut willows for baskets was always a golden time, and the soul of the weather went into the wood. If you had ever owned one of Seyavi's golden russet cooking bowls with the pattern of plumed quail, you would understand all this without saying anything.

Before Seyavi made baskets for the satisfaction of desire,—for that is a house-bred theory of art that makes anything more of it,—she danced and dressed her hair. In those days, when the spring was at flood and the blood pricked to the mating fever, the maids chose their flowers, wreathed themselves, and danced in the twilights, young desire crying out to young desire. They sang what the heart prompted, what the flower expressed, what boded in the mating weather.

"And what flower did you wear, Seyavi?"

"I, ah,—the white flower of twining (clematis), on my body and my hair, and so I sang:—

"I am the white flower of twining,
Little white flower by the river,
Oh, flower that twines close by the river;
Oh, trembling flower!
So trembles the maiden heart."

So sang Seyavi of the campoodie before she made baskets, and in her later days laid her arms upon her knees and laughed in them at the recollection. But it was not often she would say so much, never understanding the keen hunger I had for bits of lore and the "fool talk" of her people. She had fed her young son with meadowlarks' tongues, to make him quick of speech; but in late years was loath to admit it, though she had come through the period of unfaith in the lore of the clan with a fine appreciation of its beauty and significance.

"What good will your dead get, Seyavi, of the baskets you burn?" said I, coveting them for my own collection.

Thus Seyavi, "As much good as yours of the flowers you strew."

Oppapago looks on Waban, and Waban on Coso and the Bitter Lake, and the campoodie looks on these three; and more, it sees the beginning of winds along the foot of Coso, the gathering of clouds behind the high ridges, the spring flush, the soft spread of wild almond bloom on the mesa. These first, you understand, are the Paiute's walls, the other his furnishings. Not the wattled hut is his home, but the land, the winds, the hill front, the stream.

These he cannot duplicate at any furbisher's shop as you who live within doors, who, if your purse allows, may have the same home at Sitka and Samarcand. So you see how it is that the homesickness of an Indian is often unto death, since he gets no relief from it; neither wind nor weed nor sky-line, nor any aspect of the hills of a strange land sufficiently like his own. So it was when the government reached out for the Paiutes, they gathered into the Northern Reservation only such poor tribes as could devise no other end of their affairs. Here, all along the river, and south to Shoshone Land, live the clans who owned the earth, fallen into the deplorable condition of hangers-on. Yet you hear them laughing at the hour when they draw in to the campoodie after labor, when there is a smell of meat and the steam of the cooking pots goes up against the sun. Then the children lie with their toes in the ashes to hear tales; then they are merry, and have the joys of repletion and the nearness of their kind. They have their hills, and though jostled are sufficiently free to get some fortitude for what will come. For now you shall hear of the end of the basket maker.

In her best days Seyavi was most like Deborah, deep bosomed, broad in the hips, quick in counsel, slow of speech, esteemed of her people. This was that Seyavi who reared a man by her own hand, her own wit, and none other. When the townspeople began to take note of her—and it was some years after the war before there began to be any towns—she was then in the quick maturity of primitive women; but when I knew her she seemed already old.

Indian women do not often live to great age, though they look incredibly steeped in years. They have the wit to win sustenance from the raw material of life without intervention, but they have not the sleek look of the women whom the social organization conspires to nourish. Seyavi had somehow squeezed out of her daily round a spiritual ichor that kept the skill in her knotted fingers long after the accustomed time, but that also failed. By all counts she would have been about sixty years old when it came her turn to sit in the dust on the sunny side of the wickiup, with little strength left for anything but looking. And in time she paid the toll of the smoky huts and became blind. This is a thing so long expected by the Paiutes that when it comes they find it neither bitter nor sweet, but tolerable because common. There were three other blind women in the campoodie, withered fruit on a bough, but they had memory and speech. By noon of the sun there were never any left in the campoodie but these or some mother of weanlings, and they sat to keep the ashes warm upon the hearth. If it were cold, they burrowed in the blankets of the hut; if it were warm, they followed the shadow of the wickiup around. Stir much out of their places they hardly dared, since one might not help another; but they called, in high, old cracked voices, gossip and reminder across the ash heaps.

Then, if they have your speech or you theirs, and have an hour to spare, there are things to be learned of life not set down in any books, folk tales, famine tales, love and long-suffering and desire, but no whimpering. Now and then one or another of the blind keepers of the camp will come across to where you sit gossiping, tapping her way among the kitchen middens, guided by your voice that carries far in the clearness and stillness of mesa afternoons. But suppose you find Seyavi retired into the privacy of her blanket, you will get nothing for that day. There is no other privacy possible in a campoodie. All the processes of life are carried on out of doors or behind the thin, twig-woven walls of the wickiup, and laughter is the only corrective for behavior. Very early the Indian learns to possess his countenance in impassivity, to cover his head with his blanket. Something to wrap around him is as necessary to the Paiute as to you your closet to pray in.

So in her blanket Seyavi, sometime basket maker, sits by the unlit hearths of her tribe and digests her life, nourishing her spirit against the time of the spirit's need, for she knows in fact quite as much of these matters as you who have a larger hope, though she has none but the certainty that having borne herself courageously to this end she will not be reborn a coyote.

THE STREETS OF THE MOUNTAINS

All streets of the mountains lead to the citadel; steep or slow they go up to the core of the hills. Any trail that goes otherwhere must dip and cross, sidle and take chances. Rifts of the hills open into each other, and the high meadows are often wide enough to be called valleys by courtesy; but one keeps this distinction in mind,—valleys are the sunken places of the earth, cañons are scored out by the glacier ploughs of God. They have a better name in the Rockies for these hill-fenced open glades of pleasantness; they call them parks. Here and there in the hill country one comes upon blind gullies fronted by high stony barriers. These head also for the heart of the mountains; their distinction is that they never get anywhere.

All mountain streets have streams to thread them, or deep grooves where a stream might run. You would do well to avoid that range uncomforted by singing floods. You will find it forsaken of most things but beauty and madness and death and God. Many such lie east and north away from the mid Sierras, and quicken the imagination with the sense of purposes not revealed, but the ordinary traveler brings nothing away from them but an intolerable thirst.

The river cañons of the Sierras of the Snows are better worth while than most Broadways, though the choice of them is like the choice of streets, not very well determined by their names. There is always an amount of local history to be read in the names of mountain highways where one touches the successive waves of occupation or discovery, as in the old villages where the neighborhoods are not built but grow. Here you have the Spanish Californian in *Cero Gordo* and piñon; Symmes and Shepherd, pioneers both; Tunawai, probably Shoshone; Oak Creek, Kearsarge,—easy to fix the date of that christening,— Tinpah, Paiute that; Mist Cañon and Paddy Jack's. The streets of the west Sierras sloping toward the San Joaquin are long and winding, but from the east, my country, a day's ride carries one to the lake regions. The next day reaches the passes of the high divide, but whether one gets passage depends a little on how many have gone that road before, and much on one's own powers. The passes are steep and windy ridges, though not the highest. By two and three thousand feet the snow-caps overtop them. It is even possible to win through the Sierras without having passed above timber-line, but one misses a great exhilaration.

The shape of a new mountain is roughly pyramidal, running out into long shark-finned ridges that interfere and merge into other thunder-splintered sierras. You get the saw-tooth effect from a distance, but the near-by granite bulk glitters with the terrible keen polish of old glacial ages. I say terrible; so it seems. When those glossy domes swim into the alpenglow, wet after rain, you conceive how long and imperturbable are the purposes of God.

Never believe what you are told, that midsummer is the best time to go up the streets of the mountain—well—perhaps for the merely idle or sportsmanly or scientific; but for seeing and understanding, the best time is when you have the longest leave to stay. And here is a hint if you would attempt the stateliest approaches; travel light, and as much as possible live off the land. Mulligatawny soup and tinned lobster will not bring you the favor of the woodlanders.

Every cañon commends itself for some particular pleasantness; this for pines, another for trout, one for pure bleak beauty of granite buttresses, one for its far-flung irised falls; and as I say, though some are easier going, leads each to the cloud shouldering citadel. First, near the cañon mouth you get the low-heading full-branched, one-leaf pines. That is the sort of tree to know at sight, for the globose, resin-dripping cones have palatable, nourishing kernels, the main harvest of the Paiutes. That perhaps accounts for their growing accommodatingly below the limit of deep snows, grouped sombrely on the valley-ward slopes. The real procession of the pines begins in the rifts with the long-leafed *Pinus Jeffreyi*, sighing its soul away upon the wind. And it ought not to sigh in such good company. Here begins the manzanita, adjusting its tortuous stiff stems to the sharp waste of boulders, its pale olive leaves twisting edgewise to the sleek, ruddy, chestnut stems; begins also the meadowsweet, burnished laurel, and the million unregarded trumpets of the coral-red pentstemon. Wild life is likely to be busiest about the lower pine borders. One looks in hollow trees and hiving rocks for wild honey. The drone of bees, the chatter of jays, the hurry and stir of squirrels, is incessant; the air is odorous and hot. The roar of the stream fills up the morning and evening intervals, and at night the deer feed in the buckthorn thickets. It is worth watching the year round in the purlieus of the long-leafed pines. One month or another you get sight or trail of most roving mountain dwellers as they follow the limit of forbidding snows, and more bloom than you can properly appreciate.

Whatever goes up or comes down the streets of the mountains, water has the right of way; it takes the lowest ground and the shortest passage. Where the rifts are narrow, and some of the Sierra cañons are not a stone's throw from wall to wall, the best trail for foot or horse winds considerably above the watercourses; but in a country of cone-bearers there is usually a good strip of swardy sod along the cañon floor. Pine woods, the short-leafed Balfour and Murryana of the high Sierras, are sombre, rooted in the litter of a thousand years, hushed, and corrective to the spirit. The trail passes insensibly into them from the black pines and a thin belt of firs. You look back as you rise, and strain for glimpses of the tawny valley, blue glints of the Bitter Lake, and tender cloud films on the farther ranges. For such pictures the pine branches make a noble frame. Presently they close in wholly; they draw mysteriously near, covering your tracks, giving up the trail indifferently, or with a secret grudge. You get a kind of impatience with their locked ranks, until you come out lastly on some high, windy dome and see what they are about. They troop thickly up the open ways, river banks, and brook borders; up open swales of dribbling springs; swarm over old moraines; circle the peaty swamps and part and meet about clean still lakes; scale the stony gullies; tormented, bowed, persisting to the door of the storm chambers, tall priests to pray for rain. The spring winds lift clouds of pollen dust, finer than frankincense, and trail it out over high altars, staining the snow. No doubt they understand this work better than we; in fact they know no other.

"Come," say the churches of the valleys, after a season of dry years, "let us pray for rain." They would do better to plant more trees.

It is a pity we have let the gift of lyric improvisation die out. Sitting islanded on some gray peak above the encompassing wood, the soul is lifted up to sing the Iliad of the pines. They have no voice but the wind, and no sound of them rises up to the high places. But the waters, the evidences of their power, that go down the steep and stony ways, the outlets of ice-bordered pools, the young rivers swaying with the force of their running, they sing and shout and trumpet at the falls, and the noise of it far outreaches the forest spires. You see from these conning towers how they call and find each other in the slender gorges; how they fumble in the meadows, needing the sheer nearing walls to give them countenance and show the way; and how the pine woods are made glad by them.

Nothing else in the streets of the mountains gives such a sense of pageantry as the conifers; other trees, if there are any, are home dwellers, like the tender fluttered, sisterhood of quaking asp. They grow in clumps by spring borders, and all their stems have a permanent curve toward the down slope, as you may also see in hillside pines, where they have borne the weight of sagging drifts.

Well up from the valley, at the confluence of cañons, are delectable summer meadows. Fireweed flames about them against the gray boulders; streams are open, go smoothly about the glacier slips and make deep bluish pools for trout. Pines raise statelier shafts and give themselves room to grow,—gentians, shinleaf, and little grass of Parnassus in their golden checkered shadows; the meadow is white with violets and all outdoors keeps the clock. For example, when the ripples at the ford of the creek raise a clear half tone,—sign that the snow water has come down from the heated high ridges,—it is time to light the evening fire. When it drops off a note—but you will not know it except the Douglas squirrel tells you with his high, fluty chirrup from the pines' aerial gloom—sign that some star watcher has caught the first far glint of the nearing sun. Whitney cries it from his vantage tower; it flashes from Oppapago to the front of Williamson; LeConte speeds it to the westering peaks. The high rills wake and run, the birds begin. But down three thousand feet in the cañon, where you stir the fire under the cooking pot, it will not be day for an hour. It goes on, the play of light across the high places, rosy, purpling, tender, glint and glow, thunder and windy flood, like the grave, exulting talk of elders above a merry game.

Who shall say what another will find most to his liking in the streets of the mountains. As for me, once set above the country of the silver firs, I must go on until I find white columbine. Around the amphitheatres of the lake regions and above them to the limit of perennial drifts they gather flock-wise in splintered rock wastes. The crowds of them, the airy spread of sepals, the pale purity of the petal spurs, the quivering swing of bloom, obsesses the sense. One must learn to spare a little of the pang of inexpressible beauty, not to spend all one's purse in one shop. There is always another year, and another.

Lingering on in the alpine regions until the first full snow, which is often before the cessation of bloom, one goes down in good company. First snows are soft and clogging and make laborious paths. Then it is the roving inhabitants range down to the edge of the wood, below the limit of early storms. Early winter and early spring one may have sight or track of deer and bear and bighorn, cougar and bobcat, about the thickets of buckthorn on open slopes between the black pines. But when the ice crust is firm above the twenty foot drifts, they range far and forage where they will. Often in midwinter will come, now and then, a long fall of soft snow piling three or four feet above the ice crust, and work a real hardship for the dwellers of these streets. When such a storm portends the weather-wise black-tail will go down across the valley and up to the pastures of Waban where no more snow falls than suffices to nourish the sparsely growing pines. But the bighorn, the wild sheep, able to bear the bitterest storms with no signs of stress, cannot cope with the loose shifty snow. Never such a storm goes over the mountains that the Indians do not catch them floundering belly deep among the lower rifts. I have a pair of horns, inconceivably heavy, that were borne as late as a year ago by a very monarch of the flock whom death overtook at the mouth of Oak Creek after a week of wet snow. He met it as a king should, with no vain effort or trembling, and it was wholly kind to take him so with four of his following rather than that the night prowlers should find him.

There is always more life abroad in the winter hills than one looks to find, and much more in evidence than in summer weather. Light feet of hare that make no print on the forest litter leave a wondrously plain track in the snow. We used to look and look at the beginning of winter for the birds to come down from the pine lands; looked in the orchard and stubble; looked north and south on the mesa for their migratory passing, and wondered that they never came. Busy little grosbeaks picked about the kitchen doors, and woodpeckers tapped the eves of the farm buildings, but we saw hardly any other of the frequenters of the summer cañons. After a while when we grew bold to tempt the snow borders we found them in the street of the mountains. In the thick pine woods where the overlapping boughs hung with snow-wreaths make wind-proof shelter tents, in a very community of dwelling, winter the bird-folk who get their living from the persisting cones and the larvae harboring bark. Ground inhabiting species seek the dim snow chambers of the chaparral. Consider how it must be in a hill-slope overgrown with stout-twigged, partly evergreen shrubs, more than man high, and as thick as a hedge. Not all the cañon's sifting of snow can fill the intricate spaces of the hill tangles. Here and there an overhanging rock, or a stiff arch of buckthorn, makes an opening to communicating rooms and runways deep under the snow.

The light filtering through the snow walls is blue and ghostly, but serves to show seeds of shrubs and grass, and berries, and the wind-built walls are warm against the wind. It seems that live plants, especially if they are evergreen and growing, give off heat; the snow wall melts earliest from within and hollows to thinness before there is a hint of spring in the air. But you think of these things afterward. Up in the street it has the effect of being done consciously; the buckthorns lean to each other and the drift to them, the little birds run in and out of their appointed ways with the greatest cheerfulness. They give almost no tokens of distress, and even if the winter tries them too much you are not to pity them. You of the house habit can hardly understand the sense of the hills. No doubt the labor of being comfortable gives you an exaggerated opinion of yourself, an exaggerated pain to be set aside. Whether the wild things understand it or not they adapt themselves to its processes with the greater ease. The business that goes on in the street of the mountain is tremendous, world-formative. Here go birds, squirrels, and red deer, children crying small wares and playing in the street, but they do not obstruct its affairs. Summer is their holiday; "Come now," says the lord of the street, "I have need of a great work and no more playing."

But they are left borders and breathing-space out of pure kindness. They are not pushed out except by the exigencies of the nobler plan which they accept with a dignity the rest of us have not yet learned.

WATER BORDERS

I like that name the Indians give to the mountain of Lone Pine, and find it pertinent to my subject,—Oppapago, The Weeper. It sits eastward and solitary from the lordliest ranks of the Sierras, and above a range of little, old, blunt hills, and has a bowed, grave aspect as of some woman you might have known, looking out across the grassy barrows of her dead. From twin gray lakes under its noble brow stream down incessant white and tumbling waters. "Mahala all time cry," said Winnenap', drawing furrows in his rugged, wrinkled cheeks.

The origin of mountain streams is like the origin of tears, patent to the understanding but mysterious to the sense.

They are always at it, but one so seldom catches them in the act. Here in the valley there is no cessation of waters even in the season when the niggard frost gives them scant leave to run. They make the most of their midday hour, and tinkle all night thinly under the ice. An ear laid to the snow catches a muffled hint of their eternal busyness fifteen or twenty feet under the cañon drifts, and long before any appreciable spring thaw, the sagging edges of the snow bridges mark out the place of their running. One who ventures to look for it finds the immediate source of the spring freshets—all the hill fronts furrowed with the reek of melting drifts, all the gravelly flats in a swirl of waters. But later, in June or July, when the camping season begins, there runs the stream away full and singing, with no visible reinforcement other than an icy trickle from some high, belated clot of snow. Oftenest the stream drops bodily from the bleak bowl of some alpine lake; sometimes breaks out of a hillside as a spring where the ear can trace it under the rubble of loose stones to the neighborhood of some blind pool. But that leaves the lakes to be accounted for.

The lake is the eye of the mountain, jade green, placid, unwinking, also unfathomable. Whatever goes on under the high and stony brows is guessed at. It is always a favorite local tradition that one or another of the blind lakes is bottomless. Often they lie in such deep cairns of broken boulders that one never gets quite to them, or gets away unhurt. One such drops below the plunging slope that the Kearsarge trail winds over, perilously, nearing the pass. It lies still and wickedly green in its sharp-lipped cup, and the guides of that region love to tell of the packs and pack animals it has swallowed up.

But the lakes of Oppapago are perhaps not so deep, less green than gray, and better befriended. The ousel haunts them, while still hang about their coasts the thin undercut drifts that never quite leave the high altitudes. In and out of the bluish ice caves he flits and sings, and his singing heard from above is sweet and uncanny like the Nixie's chord. One finds butterflies, too, about these high, sharp regions which might be called desolate, but will not by me who love them. This is above timber-line but not too high for comforting by succulent small herbs and golden tufted grass. A granite mountain does not crumble with alacrity, but once resolved to soil makes the best of it. Every handful of loose gravel not wholly water leached affords a plant footing, and even in such unpromising surroundings there is a choice of locations. There is never going to be any communism of mountain herbage, their affinities are too sure. Full in the runnels of snow water on gravelly, open spaces in the shadow of a drift, one looks to find buttercups, frozen knee-deep by night, and owning no desire but to ripen their fruit above the icy bath. Soppy little plants of the portulaca and small, fine ferns shiver under the drip of falls and in dribbling crevices. The bleaker the situation, so it is near a stream border, the better the cassiope loves it. Yet I have not found it on the polished glacier slips, but where the country rock cleaves and splinters in the high windy headlands that the wild sheep frequents, hordes and hordes of the white bells swing over matted, mossy foliage. On Oppapago, which is also called Sheep Mountain, one finds not far from the beds of cassiope the ice-worn, stony hollows where the bighorns cradle their young. These are above the wolf's quest and the eagle's wont, and though the heather beds are softer, they are neither so dry nor so warm, and here only the stars go by. No other animal of any pretensions makes a habitat of the alpine regions. Now and then one gets a hint of some small, brown creature, rat or mouse kind, that slips secretly among the rocks; no others adapt themselves to desertness of aridity or altitude so readily as these ground inhabiting, graminivorous species. If there is an open stream the trout go up the lake as far as the water breeds food for them, but the ousel goes farthest, for pure love of it.

Since no lake can be at the highest point, it is possible to find plant life higher than the water borders; grasses perhaps the highest, gilias, royal blue trusses of polymonium, rosy plats of Sierra primroses. What one has to get used to in flowers at high altitudes is the bleaching of the sun. Hardly do they hold their virgin color for a day, and this early fading before their function is performed gives them a pitiful appearance not according with their hardihood. The color scheme runs along the high ridges from blue to rosy purple, carmine and coral red; along the water borders it is chiefly white and yellow where the mimulus makes a vivid note, running into red when the two schemes meet and mix about the borders of the meadows, at the upper limit of the columbine.

Here is the fashion in which a mountain stream gets down from the perennial pastures of the snow to its proper level and identity as an irrigating ditch. It slips stilly by the glacier scoured rim of an ice bordered pool, drops over sheer, broken ledges to another pool, gathers itself, plunges headlong on a rocky ripple slope, finds a lake again, reinforced, roars downward to a pot-hole, foams and bridles, glides a tranquil reach in some still meadow, tumbles into a sharp groove between hill flanks, curdles under the stream tangles, and so arrives at the open country and steadier going. Meadows, little strips of alpine freshness, begin before the timber-line is reached. Here one treads on a carpet of dwarf willows, downy catkins of creditable size and the greatest economy of foliage and stems. No other plant of high altitudes knows its business so well.

It hugs the ground, grows roots from stem joints where no roots should be, grows a slender leaf or two and twice as many erect full catkins that rarely, even in that short growing season, fail of fruit. Dipping over banks in the inlets of the creeks, the fortunate find the rosy apples of the miniature manzanita, barely, but always quite sufficiently, borne above the spongy sod. It does not do to be anything but humble in the alpine regions, but not fearful. I have pawed about for hours in the chill sward of meadows where one might properly expect to get one's death, and got no harm from it, except it might be Oliver Twist's complaint. One comes soon after this to shrubby willows, and where willows are trout may be confidently looked for in most Sierra streams. There is no accounting for their distribution; though provident anglers have assisted nature of late, one still comes upon roaring brown waters where trout might very well be, but are not.

The highest limit of conifers—in the middle Sierras, the white bark pine—is not along the water border. They come to it about the level of the heather, but they have no such affinity for dampness as the tamarack pines. Scarcely any bird-note breaks the stillness of the timber-line, but chipmunks inhabit here, as may be guessed by the gnawed ruddy cones of the pines, and lowering hours the woodchucks come down to the water. On a little spit of land running into Windy Lake we found one summer the evidence of a tragedy; a pair of sheep's horns not fully grown caught in the crotch of a pine where the living sheep must have lodged them. The trunk of the tree had quite closed over them, and the skull bones crumbled away from the weathered horn cases. We hoped it was not too far out of the running of night prowlers to have put a speedy end to the long agony, but we could not be sure. I never liked the spit of Windy Lake again. It seems that all snow nourished plants count nothing so excellent in their kind as to be forehanded with their bloom, working secretly to that end under the high piled winters. The heathers begin by the lake borders, while little sodden drifts still shelter under their branches. I have seen the tiniest of them (*Kalmia glauca*) blooming, and with well-formed fruit, a foot away from a snowbank from which it could hardly have emerged within a week. Somehow the soul of the heather has entered into the blood of the English-speaking.

"And oh! is that heather?" they say; and the most indifferent ends by picking a sprig of it in a hushed, wondering way. One must suppose that the root of their respective races issued from the glacial borders at about the same epoch, and remember their origin.

Among the pines where the slope of the land allows it, the streams run into smooth, brown, trout-abounding rills across open flats that are in reality filled lake basins. These are the displaying grounds of the gentians—blue—blue—eye-blue, perhaps, virtuous and likable flowers. One is not surprised to learn that they have tonic properties. But if your meadow should be outside the forest reserve, and the sheep have been there, you will find little but the shorter, paler *G. Newberryii*, and in the matted sods of the little tongues of greenness that lick up among the pines along the watercourses, white, scentless, nearly stemless, alpine violets.

At about the nine thousand foot level and in the summer there will be hosts of rosy-winged dodecatheon, called shooting-stars, outlining the crystal runnels in the sod. Single flowers have often a two-inch spread of petal, and the full, twelve blossomed heads above the slender pedicels have the airy effect of wings.

It is about this level one looks to find the largest lakes with thick ranks of pines bearing down on them, often swamped in the summer floods and paying the inevitable penalty for such encroachment. Here in wet coves of the hills harbors that crowd of bloom that makes the wonder of the Sierra cañons.

They drift under the alternate flicker and gloom of the windy rooms of pines, in gray rock shelters, and by the ooze of blind springs, and their juxtapositions are the best imaginable. Lilies come up out of fern beds, columbine swings over meadowsweet, white rein-orchids quake in the leaning grass. Open swales, where in wet years may be running water, are plantations of false hellebore (*Veratrum Californicum*), tall, branched candelabra of greenish bloom above the sessile, sheathing, boat-shaped leaves, semi-translucent in the sun. A stately plant of the lily family, but why "false?" It is frankly offensive in its character, and its young juices deadly as any hellebore that ever grew.

Like most mountain herbs it has an uncanny haste to bloom. One hears by night, when all the wood is still, the crepitatious rustle of the unfolding leaves and the pushing flower-stalk within, that has open blossoms before it has fairly uncramped from the sheath. It commends itself by a certain exclusiveness of growth, taking enough room and never elbowing; for if the flora of the lake region has a fault it is that there is too much of it. We have more than three hundred species from Kearsarge Cañon alone, and if that does not include them all it is because they were already collected otherwhere.

One expects to find lakes down to about nine thousand feet, leading into each other by comparatively open ripple slopes and white cascades. Below the lakes are filled basins that are still spongy swamps, or substantial meadows, as they get down and down.

Here begin the stream tangles. On the east slopes of the middle Sierras the pines, all but an occasional yellow variety, desert the stream borders about the level of the lowest lakes, and the birches and tree-willows begin. The firs hold on almost to the mesa levels,—there are no foothills on this eastern slope,—and whoever has firs misses nothing else. It goes without saying that a tree that can afford to take fifty years to its first fruiting will repay acquaintance. It keeps, too, all that half century, a virginal grace of outline, but having once flowered, begins quietly to put away the things of its youth. Year by year the lower rounds of boughs are shed, leaving no scar; year by year the star-branched minarets approach the sky. A fir-tree loves a water border, loves a long wind in a draughty cañon, loves to spend itself secretly on the inner finishings of its burnished, shapely cones. Broken open in mid-season the petal-shaped scales show a crimson satin surface, perfect as a rose.

The birch—the brown-bark western birch characteristic of lower stream tangles—is a spoil sport. It grows thickly to choke the stream that feeds it; grudges it the sky and space for angler's rod and fly. The willows do better; painted-cup, cypripedium, and the hollow stalks of span-broad white umbels, find a footing among their stems. But in general the steep plunges, the white swirls, green and tawny pools, the gliding hush of waters between the meadows and the mesas afford little fishing and few flowers.

One looks for these to begin again when once free of the rifted cañon walls; the high note of babble and laughter falls off to the steadier mellow tone of a stream that knows its purpose and reflects the sky.

OTHER WATER BORDERS

It is the proper destiny of every considerable stream in the west to become an irrigating ditch. It would seem the streams are willing. They go as far as they can, or dare, toward the tillable lands in their own boulder fenced gullies—but how much farther in the man-made waterways. It is difficult to come into intimate relations with appropriated waters; like very busy people they have no time to reveal themselves. One needs to have known an irrigating ditch when it was a brook, and to have lived by it, to mark the morning and evening tone of its crooning, rising and falling to the excess of snow water; to have watched far across the valley, south to the Eclipse and north to the Twisted Dyke, the shining wall of the village water gate; to see still blue herons stalking the little glinting weirs across the field.

Perhaps to get into the mood of the waterways one needs to have seen old Amos Judson asquat on the headgate with his gun, guarding his water-right toward the end of a dry summer. Amos owned the half of Tule Creek and the other half pertained to the neighboring Greenfields ranch. Years of a "short water crop," that is, when too little snow fell on the high pine ridges, or, falling, melted too early, Amos held that it took all the water that came down to make his half, and maintained it with a Winchester and a deadly aim. Jesus Montaña, first proprietor of Greenfields,—you can see at once that Judson had the racial advantage,—contesting the right with him, walked into five of Judson's bullets and his eternal possessions on the same occasion. That was the Homeric age of settlement and passed into tradition. Twelve years later one of the Clarks, holding Greenfields, not so very green by now, shot one of the Judsons. Perhaps he hoped that also might become classic, but the jury found for manslaughter. It had the effect of discouraging the Greenfields claim, but Amos used to sit on the headgate just the same, as quaint and lone a figure as the sandhill crane watching for water toads below the Tule drop. Every subsequent owner of Greenfields bought it with Amos in full view. The last of these was Diedrick. Along in August of that year came a week of low water. Judson's ditch failed and he went out with his rifle to learn why. There on the headgate sat Diedrick's frau with a long-handled shovel across her lap and all the water turned into Diedrick's ditch; there she sat knitting through the long sun, and the children brought out her dinner. It was all up with Amos; he was too much of a gentleman to fight a lady—that was the way he expressed it. She was a very large lady, and a long-handled shovel is no mean weapon. The next year Judson and Diedrick put in a modern water gauge and took the summer ebb in equal inches. Some of the water-right difficulties are more squalid than this, some more tragic; but unless you have known them you cannot very well know what the water thinks as it slips past the gardens and in the long slow sweeps of the canal. You get that sense of brooding from the confined and sober floods, not all at once but by degrees, as one might become aware of a middle-aged and serious neighbor who has had that in his life to make him so. It is the repose of the completely accepted instinct.

With the water runs a certain following of thirsty herbs and shrubs. The willows go as far as the stream goes, and a bit farther on the slightest provocation. They will strike root in the leak of a flume, or the dribble of an overfull bank, coaxing the water beyond its appointed bounds. Given a new waterway in a barren land, and in three years the willows have fringed all its miles of banks; three years more and they will touch tops across it. It is perhaps due to the early usurpation of the willows that so little else finds growing-room along the large canals. The birch beginning far back in the cañon tangles is more conservative; it is shy of man haunts and needs to have the permanence of its drink assured. It stops far short of the summer limit of waters, and I have never known it to take up a position on the banks beyond the ploughed lands. There is something almost like premeditation in the avoidance of cultivated tracts by certain plants of water borders. The clematis, mingling its foliage secretly with its host, comes down with the stream tangles to the village fences, skips over to corners of little used pasture lands and the plantations that spring up about waste water pools; but never ventures a footing in the trail of spade or plough; will not be persuaded to grow in any garden plot. On the other hand, the horehound, the common European species imported with the colonies, hankers after hedgerows and snug little borders. It is more widely distributed than many native species, and may be always found along the ditches in the village corners, where it is not appreciated.

The irrigating ditch is an impartial distributer. It gathers all the alien weeds that come west in garden and grass seeds and affords them harbor in its banks. There one finds the European mallow *(Malva rotundifolia)* spreading out to the streets with the summer overflow, and every spring a dandelion or two, brought in with the blue grass seed, uncurls in the swardy soil. Farther than either of these have come the lilies that the Chinese coolies cultivate in adjacent mud holes for their foodful bulbs. The *seegoo* establishes itself very readily in swampy borders, and the white blossom spikes among the arrow-pointed leaves are quite as acceptable to the eye as any native species.

In the neighborhood of towns founded by the Spanish Californians, whether this plant is native to the locality or not, one can always find aromatic clumps of *yerba buena*, the "good herb" *(Micromeria Douglassii)*. The virtue of it as a febrifuge was taught to the mission fathers by the neophytes, and wise old dames of my acquaintance have worked astonishing cures with it and the succulent *yerba mansa*. This last is native to wet meadows and distinguished enough to have a family all to itself.

Where the irrigating ditches are shallow and a little neglected, they choke quickly with watercress that multiplies about the lowest Sierra springs. It is characteristic of the frequenters of water borders near man haunts, that they are chiefly of the sorts that are useful to man, as if they made their services an excuse for the intrusion. The joint-grass of soggy pastures produces edible, nut-flavored tubers, called by the Indians *taboose*. The common reed of the ultramontane marshes (here *Phragmites vulgaris*), a very stately, whispering reed, light and strong for shafts or arrows, affords sweet sap and pith which makes a passable sugar.

It seems the secrets of plant powers and influences yield themselves most readily to primitive peoples, at least one never hears of the knowledge coming from any other source. The Indian never concerns himself, as the botanist and the poet, with the plant's appearances and relations, but with what it can do for him. It can do much, but how do you suppose he finds it out; what instincts or accidents guide him? How does a cat know when to eat catnip? Why do western bred cattle avoid loco weed, and strangers eat it and go mad? One might suppose that in a time of famine the Paiutes digged wild parsnip in meadow corners and died from eating it, and so learned to produce death swiftly and at will. But how did they learn, repenting in the last agony, that animal fat is the best antidote for its virulence; and who taught them that the essence of joint pine (*Ephedra nevadensis*), which looks to have no juice in it of any sort, is efficacious in stomachic disorders. But they so understand and so use. One believes it to be a sort of instinct atrophied by disuse in a complexer civilization. I remember very well when I came first upon a wet meadow of *yerba mansa*, not knowing its name or use. It *looked* potent; the cool, shiny leaves, the succulent, pink stems and fruity bloom. A little touch, a hint, a word, and I should have known what use to put them to. So I felt, unwilling to leave it until we had come to an understanding. So a musician might have felt in the presence of an instrument known to be within his province, but beyond his power. It was with the relieved sense of having shaped a long surmise that I watched the Senora Romero make a poultice of it for my burned hand.

On, down from the lower lakes to the village weirs, the brown and golden disks of *helenum* have beauty as a sufficient excuse for being. The plants anchor out on tiny capes, or mid-stream islets, with the nearly sessile radicle leaves submerged. The flowers keep up a constant trepidation in time with the hasty water beating at their stems, a quivering, instinct with life, that seems always at the point of breaking into flight; just as the babble of the watercourses always approaches articulation but never quite achieves it. Although of wide range the helenum never makes itself common through profusion, and may be looked for in the same places from year to year. Another lake dweller that comes down to the ploughed lands is the red columbine (*C. truncata*). It requires no encouragement other than shade, but grows too rank in the summer heats and loses its wildwood grace. A common enough orchid in these parts is the false lady's slipper (*Epipactis gigantea*), one that springs up by any water where there is sufficient growth of other sorts to give it countenance. It seems to thrive best in an atmosphere of suffocation.

The middle Sierras fall off abruptly eastward toward the high valleys. Peaks of the fourteen thousand class, belted with sombre swathes of pine, rise almost directly from the bench lands with no foothill approaches. At the lower edge of the bench or mesa the land falls away, often by a fault, to the river hollows, and along the drop one looks for springs or intermittent swampy swales. Here the plant world resembles a little the lake gardens, modified by altitude and the use the town folk put it to for pasture. Here are cress, blue violets, potentilla, and, in the damp of the willow fence-rows, white false asphodels. I am sure we make too free use of this word *false* in naming plants—false mallow, false lupine, and the like. The asphodel is at least no falsifier, but a true lily by all the heaven-set marks, though small of flower and run mostly to leaves, and should have a name that gives it credit for growing up in such celestial semblance. Native to the mesa meadows is a pale iris, gardens of it acres wide, that in the spring season of full bloom make an airy fluttering as of azure wings. Single flowers are too thin and sketchy of outline to affect the imagination, but the full fields have the misty blue of mirage waters rolled across desert sand, and quicken the senses to the anticipation of things ethereal. A very poet's flower, I thought; not fit for gathering up, and proving a nuisance in the pastures, therefore needing to be the more loved. And one day I caught Winnenap' drawing out from mid leaf a fine strong fibre for making snares. The borders of the iris fields are pure gold, nearly sessile buttercups and a creeping-stemmed composite of a redder hue. I am convinced that English-speaking children will always have buttercups. If they do not light upon the original companion of little frogs they will take the next best and cherish it accordingly. I find five unrelated species loved by that name, and as many more and as inappropriately called cowslips.

By every mesa spring one may expect to find a single shrub of the buckthorn, called of old time *Cascara sagrada*—the sacred bark. Up in the cañons, within the limit of the rains, it seeks rather a stony slope, but in the dry valleys is not found away from water borders.

In all the valleys and along the desert edges of the west are considerable areas of soil sickly with alkali-collecting pools, black and evil-smelling like old blood. Very little grows hereabout but thick-leaved pickle weed. Curiously enough, in this stiff mud, along roadways where there is frequently a little leakage from canals, grows the only western representative of the true heliotropes (*Heliotropium curassavicum*). It has flowers of faded white, foliage of faded green, resembling the "live-for-ever" of old gardens and graveyards, but even less attractive. After so much schooling in the virtues of water-seeking plants, one is not surprised to learn that its mucilaginous sap has healing powers.

Last and inevitable resort of overflow waters is the tulares, great wastes of reeds (*Juncus*) in sickly, slow streams. The reeds, called tules, are ghostly pale in winter, in summer deep poisonous-looking green, the waters thick and brown; the reed beds breaking into dingy pools, clumps of rotting willows, narrow winding water lanes and sinking paths. The tules grow inconceivably thick in places, standing man-high above the water; cattle, no, not any fish nor fowl can penetrate them. Old stalks succumb slowly; the bed soil is quagmire, settling with the weight as it fills and fills. Too slowly for counting they raise little islands from the bog and reclaim the land. The waters pushed out cut deeper channels, gnaw off the edges of the solid earth.

The tulares are full of mystery and malaria. That is why we have meant to explore them and have never done so. It must be a happy mystery. So you would think to hear the redwinged blackbirds proclaim it clear March mornings. Flocks of them, and every flock a myriad, shelter in the dry, whispering stems. They make little arched runways deep into the heart of the tule beds. Miles across the valley one hears the clamor of their high, keen flutings in the mating weather.

Wild fowl, quacking hordes of them, nest in the tulares. Any day's venture will raise from open shallows the great blue heron on his hollow wings. Chill evenings the mallard drakes cry continually from the glassy pools, the bittern's hollow boom rolls along the water paths. Strange and far-flown fowl drop down against the saffron, autumn sky. All day wings beat above it hazy with speed; long flights of cranes glimmer in the twilight. By night one wakes to hear the clanging geese go over. One wishes for, but gets no nearer speech from those the reedy fens have swallowed up. What they do there, how fare, what find, is the secret of the tulares.

NURSLINGS OF THE SKY

Choose a hill country for storms. There all the business of the weather is carried on above your horizon and loses its terror in familiarity. When you come to think about it, the disastrous storms are on the levels, sea or sand or plains. There you get only a hint of what is about to happen, the fume of the gods rising from their meeting place under the rim of the world; and when it breaks upon you there is no stay nor shelter. The terrible mewings and mouthings of a Kansas wind have the added terror of viewlessness. You are lapped in them like uprooted grass; suspect them of a personal grudge. But the storms of hill countries have other business. They scoop watercourses, manure the pines, twist them to a finer fibre, fit the firs to be masts and spars, and, if you keep reasonably out of the track of their affairs, do you no harm.

They have habits to be learned, appointed paths, seasons, and warnings, and they leave you in no doubt about their performances. One who builds his house on a water scar or the rubble of a steep slope must take chances. So they did in Overtown who built in the wash of Argus water, and at Kearsarge at the foot of a steep, treeless swale. After twenty years Argus water rose in the wash against the frail houses, and the piled snows of Kearsarge slid down at a thunder peal over the cabins and the camp, but you could conceive that it was the fault of neither the water nor the snow.

The first effect of cloud study is a sense of presence and intention in storm processes.

Weather does not happen. It is the visible manifestation of the Spirit moving itself in the void. It gathers itself together under the heavens; rains, snows, yearns mightily in wind, smiles; and the Weather Bureau, situated advantageously for that very business, taps the record on his instruments and going out on the streets denies his God, not having gathered the sense of what he has seen. Hardly anybody takes account of the fact that John Muir, who knows more of mountain storms than any other, is a devout man.

Of the high Sierras choose the neighborhood of the splintered peaks about the Kern and King's river divide for storm study, or the short, wide-mouthed cañons opening eastward on high valleys. Days when the hollows are steeped in a warm, winey flood the clouds come walking on the floor of heaven, flat and pearly gray beneath, rounded and pearly white above. They gather flock-wise, moving on the level currents that roll about the peaks, lock hands and settle with the cooler air, drawing a veil about those places where they do their work. If their meeting or parting takes place at sunrise or sunset, as it often does, one gets the splendor of the apocalypse. There will be cloud pillars miles high, snow-capped, glorified, and preserving an orderly perspective before the unbarred door of the sun, or perhaps mere ghosts of clouds that dance to some pied piper of an unfelt wind. But be it day or night, once they have settled to their work, one sees from the valley only the blank wall of their tents stretched along the ranges. To get the real effect of a mountain storm you must be inside.

One who goes often into a hill country learns not to say: What if it should rain? It always does rain somewhere among the peaks: the unusual thing is that one should escape it. You might suppose that if you took any account of plant contrivances to save their pollen powder against showers. Note how many there are deep-throated and bell-flowered like the pentstemons, how many have nodding pedicels as the columbine, how many grow in copse shelters and grow there only. There is keen delight in the quick showers of summer cañons, with the added comfort, born of experience, of knowing that no harm comes of a wetting at high altitudes. The day is warm; a white cloud spies over the cañon wall, slips up behind the ridge to cross it by some windy pass, obscures your sun. Next you hear the rain drum on the broad-leaved hellebore, and beat down the mimulus beside the brook. You shelter on the lee of some strong pine with shut-winged butterflies and merry, fiddling creatures of the wood. Runnels of rain water from the glacier-slips swirl through the pine needles into rivulets; the streams froth and rise in their banks. The sky is white with cloud; the sky is gray with rain; the sky is clear. The summer showers leave no wake.

Such as these follow each other day by day for weeks in August weather. Sometimes they chill suddenly into wet snow that packs about the lake gardens clear to the blossom frills, and melts away harmlessly. Sometimes one has the good fortune from a heather—grown headland to watch a rain-cloud forming in mid-air. Out over meadow or lake region begins a little darkling of the sky,—no cloud, no wind, just a smokiness such as spirits materialize from in witch stories.

It rays out and draws to it some floating films from secret cañons. Rain begins, "slow dropping veil of thinnest lawn;" a wind comes up and drives the formless thing across a meadow, or a dull lake pitted by the glancing drops, dissolving as it drives. Such rains relieve like tears.

The same season brings the rains that have work to do, ploughing storms that alter the face of things. These come with thunder and the play of live fire along the rocks. They come with great winds that try the pines for their work upon the seas and strike out the unfit. They shake down avalanches of splinters from sky-line pinnacles and raise up sudden floods like battle fronts in the cañons against towns, trees, and boulders. They would be kind if they could, but have more important matters. Such storms, called cloud-bursts by the country folk, are not rain, rather the spillings of Thor's cup, jarred by the Thunderer. After such a one the water that comes up in the village hydrants miles away is white with forced bubbles from the wind-tormented streams.

All that storms do to the face of the earth you may read in the geographies, but not what they do to our contemporaries. I remember one night of thunderous rain made unendurably mournful by the houseless cry of a cougar whose lair, and perhaps his family, had been buried under a slide of broken boulders on the slope of Kearsarge. We had heard the heavy denotation of the slide about the hour of the alpenglow, a pale rosy interval in a darkling air, and judged he must have come from hunting to the ruined cliff and paced the night out before it, crying a very human woe. I remember, too, in that same season of storms, a lake made milky white for days, and crowded out of its bed by clay washed into it by a fury of rain, with the trout floating in it belly up, stunned by the shock of the sudden flood. But there were trout enough for what was left of the lake next year and the beginning of a meadow about its upper rim. What taxed me most in the wreck of one of my favorite cañons by cloudburst was to see a bobcat mother mouthing her drowned kittens in the ruined lair built in the wash, far above the limit of accustomed waters, but not far enough for the unexpected. After a time you get the point of view of gods about these things to save you from being too pitiful.

The great snows that come at the beginning of winter, before there is yet any snow except the perpetual high banks, are best worth while to watch. These come often before the late bloomers are gone and while the migratory birds are still in the piney woods. Down in the valley you see little but the flocking of blackbirds in the streets, or the low flight of mallards over the tulares, and the gathering of clouds behind Williamson. First there is a waiting stillness in the wood; the pine-trees creak although there is no wind, the sky glowers, the firs rock by the water borders. The noise of the creek rises insistently and falls off a full note like a child abashed by sudden silence in the room. This changing of the stream-tone following tardily the changes of the sun on melting snows is most meaningful of wood notes. After it runs a little trumpeter wind to cry the wild creatures to their holes. Sometimes the warning hangs in the air for days with increasing stillness. Only Clark's crow and the strident jays make light of it; only they can afford to. The cattle get down to the foothills and ground inhabiting creatures make fast their doors. It grows chill, blind clouds fumble in the cañons; there will be a roll of thunder, perhaps, or a flurry of rain, but mostly the snow is born in the air with quietness and the sense of strong white pinions softly stirred. It increases, is wet and clogging, and makes a white night of midday.

There is seldom any wind with first snows, more often rain, but later, when there is already a smooth foot or two over all the slopes, the drifts begin. The late snows are fine and dry, mere ice granules at the wind's will. Keen mornings after a storm they are blown out in wreaths and banners from the high ridges sifting into the cañons.

Once in a year or so we have a "big snow." The cloud tents are widened out to shut in the valley and an outlying range or two and are drawn tight against the sun. Such a storm begins warm, with a dry white mist that fills and fills between the ridges, and the air is thick with formless groaning. Now for days you get no hint of the neighboring ranges until the snows begin to lighten and some shouldering peak lifts through a rent. Mornings after the heavy snows are steely blue, two-edged with cold, divinely fresh and still, and these are times to go up to the pine borders. There you may find floundering in the unstable drifts "tainted wethers" of the wild sheep, faint from age and hunger; easy prey. Even the deer make slow going in the thick fresh snow, and once we found a wolverine going blind and feebly in the white glare.

No tree takes the snow stress with such ease as the silver fir. The star-whorled, fan-spread branches droop under the soft wreaths—droop and press flatly to the trunk; presently the point of overloading is reached, there is a soft sough and muffled dropping, the boughs recover, and the weighting goes on until the drifts have reached the midmost whorls and covered up the branches. When the snows are particularly wet and heavy they spread over the young firs in green-ribbed tents wherein harbor winter loving birds.

All storms of desert hills, except wind storms, are impotent. East and east of the Sierras they rise in nearly parallel ranges, desertward, and no rain breaks over them, except from some far-strayed cloud or roving wind from the California Gulf, and these only in winter. In summer the sky travails with thunderings and the flare of sheet lightnings to win a few blistering big drops, and once in a lifetime the chance of a torrent. But you have not known what force resides in the mindless things until you have known a desert wind. One expects it at the turn of the two seasons, wet and dry, with electrified tense nerves. Along the edge of the mesa where it drops off to the valley, dust devils begin to rise white and steady, fanning out at the top like the genii out of the Fisherman's bottle. One supposes the Indians might have learned the use of smoke signals from these dust pillars as they learn most things direct from the tutelage of the earth. The air begins to move fluently, blowing hot and cold between the ranges. Far south rises a murk of sand against the sky; it grows, the wind shakes itself, and has a smell of earth. The cloud of small dust takes on the color of gold and shuts out the neighborhood, the push of the wind is unsparing. Only man of all folk is foolish enough to stir abroad in it. But being in a house is really much worse; no relief from the dust, and a great fear of the creaking timbers. There is no looking ahead in such a wind, and the bite of the small sharp sand on exposed skin is keener than any insect sting. One might sleep, for the lapping of the wind wears one to the point of exhaustion very soon, but there is dread, in open sand stretches sometimes justified, of being over blown by the drift. It is hot, dry, fretful work, but by going along the ground with the wind behind, one may come upon strange things in its tumultuous privacy. I like these truces of wind and heat that the desert makes, otherwise I do not know how I should come by so many acquaintances with furtive folk. I like to see hawks sitting daunted in shallow holes, not daring to spread a feather, and doves in a row by the prickle bushes, and shut-eyed cattle, turned tail to the wind in a patient doze. I like the smother of sand among the dunes, and finding small coiled snakes in open places, but I never like to come in a wind upon the silly sheep. The wind robs them of what wit they had, and they seem never to have learned the self-induced hypnotic stupor with which most wild things endure weather stress. I have never heard that the desert winds brought harm to any other than the wandering shepherds and their flocks. Once below Pastaria Little Pete showed me bones sticking out of the sand where a flock of two hundred had been smothered in a bygone wind. In many places the four-foot posts of a cattle fence had been buried by the wind-blown dunes.

It is enough occupation, when no storm is brewing, to watch the cloud currents and the chambers of the sky. From Kearsarge, say, you look over Inyo and find pink soft cloud masses asleep on the level desert air; south of you hurries a white troop late to some gathering of their kind at the back of Oppapago; nosing the foot of Waban, a woolly mist creeps south. In the clean, smooth paths of the middle sky and highest up in air, drift, unshepherded, small flocks ranging contrarily. You will find the proper names of these things in the reports of the Weather Bureau—cirrus, cumulus, and the like—and charts that will teach by study when to sow and take up crops. It is astonishing the trouble men will be at to find out when to plant potatoes, and gloze over the eternal meaning of the skies. You have to beat out for yourself many mornings on the windly headlands the sense of the fact that you get the same rainbow in the cloud drift over Waban and the spray of your garden hose. And not necessarily then do you live up to it.

THE LITTLE TOWN OF THE GRAPE VINES

There are still some places in the west where the quails cry "*cuidado*"; where all the speech is soft, all the manners gentle; where all the dishes have *chile* in them, and they make more of the Sixteenth of September than they do of the Fourth of July. I mean in particular El Pueblo de Las Uvas. Where it lies, how to come at it, you will not get from me; rather would I show you the heron's nest in the tulares. It has a peak behind it, glinting above the tamarack pines, above a breaker of ruddy hills that have a long slope valley-wards and the shoreward steep of waves toward the Sierras.

Below the Town of the Grape Vines, which shortens to Las Uvas for common use, the land dips away to the river pastures and the tulares. It shrouds under a twilight thicket of vines, under a dome of cottonwood-trees, drowsy and murmurous as a hive. Hereabouts are some strips of tillage and the headgates that dam up the creek for the village weirs; upstream you catch the growl of the arrastra. Wild vines that begin among the willows lap over to the orchard rows, take the trellis and roof-tree.

There is another town above Las Uvas that merits some attention, a town of arches and airy crofts, full of linnets, blackbirds, fruit birds, small sharp hawks, and mockingbirds that sing by night. They pour out piercing, unendurably sweet cavatinas above the fragrance of bloom and musky smell of fruit. Singing is in fact the business of the night at Las Uvas as sleeping is for midday. When the moon comes over the mountain wall new-washed from the sea, and the shadows lie like lace on the stamped floors of the patios, from recess to recess of the vine tangle runs the thrum of guitars and the voice of singing.

At Las Uvas they keep up all the good customs brought out of Old Mexico or bred in a lotus-eating land; drink, and are merry and look out for something to eat afterward; have children, nine or ten to a family, have cock-fights, keep the siesta, smoke cigarettes and wait for the sun to go down. And always they dance; at dusk on the smooth adobe floors, afternoons under the trellises where the earth is damp and has a fruity smell. A betrothal, a wedding, or a christening, or the mere proximity of a guitar is sufficient occasion; and if the occasion lacks, send for the guitar and dance anyway.

All this requires explanation. Antonio Sevadra, drifting this way from Old Mexico with the flood that poured into the Tappan district after the first notable strike, discovered La Golondrina. It was a generous lode and Tony a good fellow; to work it he brought in all the Sevadras, even to the twice-removed; all the Castros who were his wife's family, all the Saises, Romeros, and Eschobars,—the relations of his relations-in- law. There you have the beginning of a pretty considerable town. To these accrued much of the Spanish California float swept out of the southwest by eastern enterprise. They slacked away again when the price of silver went down, and the ore dwindled in La Golondrina. All the hot eddy of mining life swept away from that corner of the hills, but there were always those too idle, too poor to move, or too easily content with El Pueblo de Las Uvas.

Nobody comes nowadays to the town of the grape vines except, as we say, "with the breath of crying," but of these enough. All the low sills run over with small heads. Ah, ah! There is a kind of pride in that if you did but know it, to have your baby every year or so as the time sets, and keep a full breast. So great a blessing as marriage is easily come by. It is told of Ruy Garcia that when he went for his marriage license he lacked a dollar of the clerk's fee, but borrowed it of the sheriff, who expected reelection and exhibited thereby a commendable thrift.

Of what account is it to lack meal or meat when you may have it of any neighbor?

Besides, there is sometimes a point of honor in these things. Jesus Romero, father of ten, had a job sacking ore in the Marionette which he gave up of his own accord. "Eh, why?" said Jesus, "for my fam'ly."

"It is so, señora," he said solemnly, "I go to the Marionette, I work, I eat meat—pie—frijoles—good, ver' good. I come home sad'day nigh' I see my fam'ly. I play lil' game poker with the boys, have lil' drink wine, my money all gone. My family have no money, nothing eat. All time I work at mine I eat, good, ver' good grub. I think sorry for my fam'ly. No, no, señora, I no work no more that Marionette, I stay with my fam'ly." The wonder of it is, I think, that the family had the same point of view.

Every house in the town of the vines has its garden plot, corn and brown beans and a row of peppers reddening in the sun; and in damp borders of the irrigating ditches clumps of *yerba santa,* horehound, catnip, and spikenard, wholesome herbs and curative, but if no peppers then nothing at all. You will have for a holiday dinner, in Las Uvas, soup with meat balls and chile in it, chicken with chile, rice with chile, fried beans with more chile, enchilada, which is corn cake with a sauce of chile and tomatoes, onion, grated cheese, and olives, and for a relish chile *tepines* passed about in a dish, all of which is comfortable and corrective to the stomach. You will have wine which every man makes for himself, of good body and inimitable bouquet, and sweets that are not nearly so nice as they look.

There are two occasions when you may count on that kind of a meal; always on the Sixteenth of September, and on the two-yearly visits of Father Shannon. It is absurd, of course, that El Pueblo de Las Uvas should have an Irish priest, but Black Rock, Minton, Jimville, and all that country round do not find it so. Father Shannon visits them all, waits by the Red Butte to confess the shepherds who go through with their flocks, carries blessing to small and isolated mines, and so in the course of a year or so works around to Las Uvas to bury and marry and christen. Then all the little graves in the *Campo Santo* are brave with tapers, the brown pine headboards blossom like Aaron's rod with paper roses and bright cheap prints of Our Lady of Sorrows. Then the Señora Sevadra, who thinks herself elect of heaven for that office, gathers up the original sinners, the little Elijias, Lolas, Manuelitas, José, and Felipés, by dint of adjurations and sweets smuggled into small perspiring palms, to fit them for the Sacrament.

I used to peek in at them, never so softly, in Dona Ina's living-room; Raphael-eyed little imps, going sidewise on their knees to rest them from the bare floor, candles lit on the mantel to give a religious air, and a great sheaf of wild bloom before the Holy Family. Come Sunday they set out the altar in the schoolhouse, with the fine-drawn altar cloths, the beaten silver candlesticks, and the wax images, chief glory of Las Uvas, brought up mule-back from Old Mexico forty years ago. All in white the communicants go up two and two in a hushed, sweet awe to take the body of their Lord, and Tomaso, who is priest's boy, tries not to look unduly puffed up by his office. After that you have dinner and a bottle of wine that ripened on the sunny slope of Escondito. All the week Father Shannon has shriven his people, who bring clean conscience to the betterment of appetite, and the Father sets them an example. Father Shannon is rather big about the middle to accommodate the large laugh that lives in him, but a most shrewd searcher of hearts. It is reported that one derives comfort from his confessional, and I for my part believe it.

The celebration of the Sixteenth, though it comes every year, takes as long to prepare for as Holy Communion. The señoritas have each a new dress apiece, the señoras a new *rebosa*. The young gentlemen have new silver trimmings to their sombreros, unspeakable ties, silk handkerchiefs, and new leathers to their spurs. At this time when the peppers glow in the gardens and the young quail cry "*cuidado*," "have a care!" you can hear the *plump, plump* of the *metate* from the alcoves of the vines where comfortable old dames, whose experience gives them the touch of art, are pounding out corn for tamales.

School-teachers from abroad have tried before now at Las Uvas to have school begin on the first of September, but got nothing else to stir in the heads of the little Castros, Garcias, and Romeros but feasts and cock-fights until after the Sixteenth. Perhaps you need to be told that this is the anniversary of the Republic, when liberty awoke and cried in the provinces of Old Mexico. You are aroused at midnight to hear them shouting in the streets, "*Vive la Libertad!*" answered from the houses and the recesses of the vines, "*Vive la Mexico!*" At sunrise shots are fired commemorating the tragedy of unhappy Maximilian, and then music, the noblest of national hymns, as the great flag of Old Mexico floats up the flag-pole in the bare little plaza of shabby Las Uvas. The sun over Pine Mountain greets the eagle of Montezuma before it touches the vineyards and the town, and the day begins with a great shout. By and by there will be a reading of the Declaration of Independence and an address punctured by *vives*; all the town in its best dress, and some exhibits of horsemanship that make lathered bits and bloodly spurs; also a cock-fight.

By night there will be dancing, and such music! old Santos to play the flute, a little lean man with a saintly countenance, young Garcia whose guitar has a soul, and Carrasco with the violin. They sit on a high platform above the dancers in the candle flare, backed by the red, white, and green of Old Mexico, and play fervently such music as you will not hear otherwhere.

At midnight the flag comes down. Count yourself at a loss if you are not moved by that performance. Pine Mountain watches whitely overhead, shepherd fires glow strongly on the glooming hills. The plaza, the bare glistening pole, the dark folk, the bright dresses, are lit ruddily by a bonfire. It leaps up to the eagle flag, dies down, the music begins softly and aside. They play airs of old longing and exile; slowly out of the dark the flag drops down, bellying and falling with the midnight draught. Sometimes a hymn is sung, always there are tears. The flag is down; Tony Sevadra has received it in his arms. The music strikes a barbaric swelling tune, another flag begins a slow ascent,—it takes a breath or two to realize that they are both, flag and tune, the Star Spangled Banner,—a volley is fired, we are back, if you please, in California of America. Every youth who has the blood of patriots in him lays ahold on Tony Sevadra's flag, happiest if he can get a corner of it. The music goes before, the folk fall in two and two, singing. They sing everything, America, the Marseillaise, for the sake of the French shepherds hereabout, the hymn of Cuba, and the Chilian national air to comfort two families of that land. The flag goes to Do±a Ina's, with the candlesticks and the altar cloths, then Las Uvas eats tamales and dances the sun up the slope of Pine Mountain.

You are not to suppose that they do not keep the Fourth, Washington's Birthday, and Thanksgiving at the town of the grape vines. These make excellent occasions for quitting work and dancing, but the Sixteenth is the holiday of the heart. On Memorial Day the graves have garlands and new pictures of the saints tacked to the headboards. There is great virtue in an *Ave* said in the Camp of the Saints. I like that name which the Spanish speaking people give to the garden of the dead, *Campo Santo,* as if it might be some bed of healing from which blind souls and sinners rise up whole and praising God. Sometimes the speech of simple folk hints at truth the understanding does not reach. I am persuaded only a complex soul can get any good of a plain religion. Your earth-born is a poet and a symbolist. We breed in an environment of asphalt pavements a body of people whose creeds are chiefly restrictions against other people's way of life, and have kitchens and latrines under the same roof that houses their God. Such as these go to church to be edified, but at Las Uvas they go for pure worship and to entreat their God. The logical conclusion of the faith that every good gift cometh from God is the open hand and the finer courtesy. The meal done without buys a candle for the neighbor's dead child. You do foolishly to suppose that the candle does no good.

At Las Uvas every house is a piece of earth—thick walled, whitewashed adobe that keeps the even temperature of a cave; every man is an accomplished horseman and consequently bow-legged; every family keeps dogs, flea-bitten mongrels that loll on the earthen floors. They speak a purer Castilian than obtains in like villages of Mexico, and the way they count relationship everybody is more or less akin. There is not much villainy among them. What incentive to thieving or killing can there be when there is little wealth and that to be had for the borrowing! If they love too hotly, as we say "take their meat before grace," so do their betters. Eh, what! shall a man be a saint before he is dead? And besides, Holy Church takes it out of you one way or another before all is done. Come away, you who are obsessed with your own importance in the scheme of things, and have got nothing you did not sweat for, come away by the brown valleys and full-bosomed hills to the even-breathing days, to the kindliness, earthiness, ease of El Pueblo de Las Uvas.

CPSIA information can be obtained
at www.ICGtesting.com
Printed in the USA
LVOW12s1530180817
545348LV00001B/19/P